THE

PEN & INK PLAYBOOK

44 Exercises to Sketch, Dip, and Drizzle with Ballpoint, Dip Pens & Ink

ANA MONTIEL

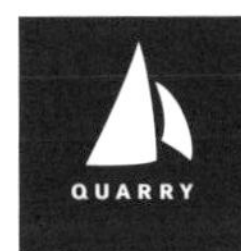

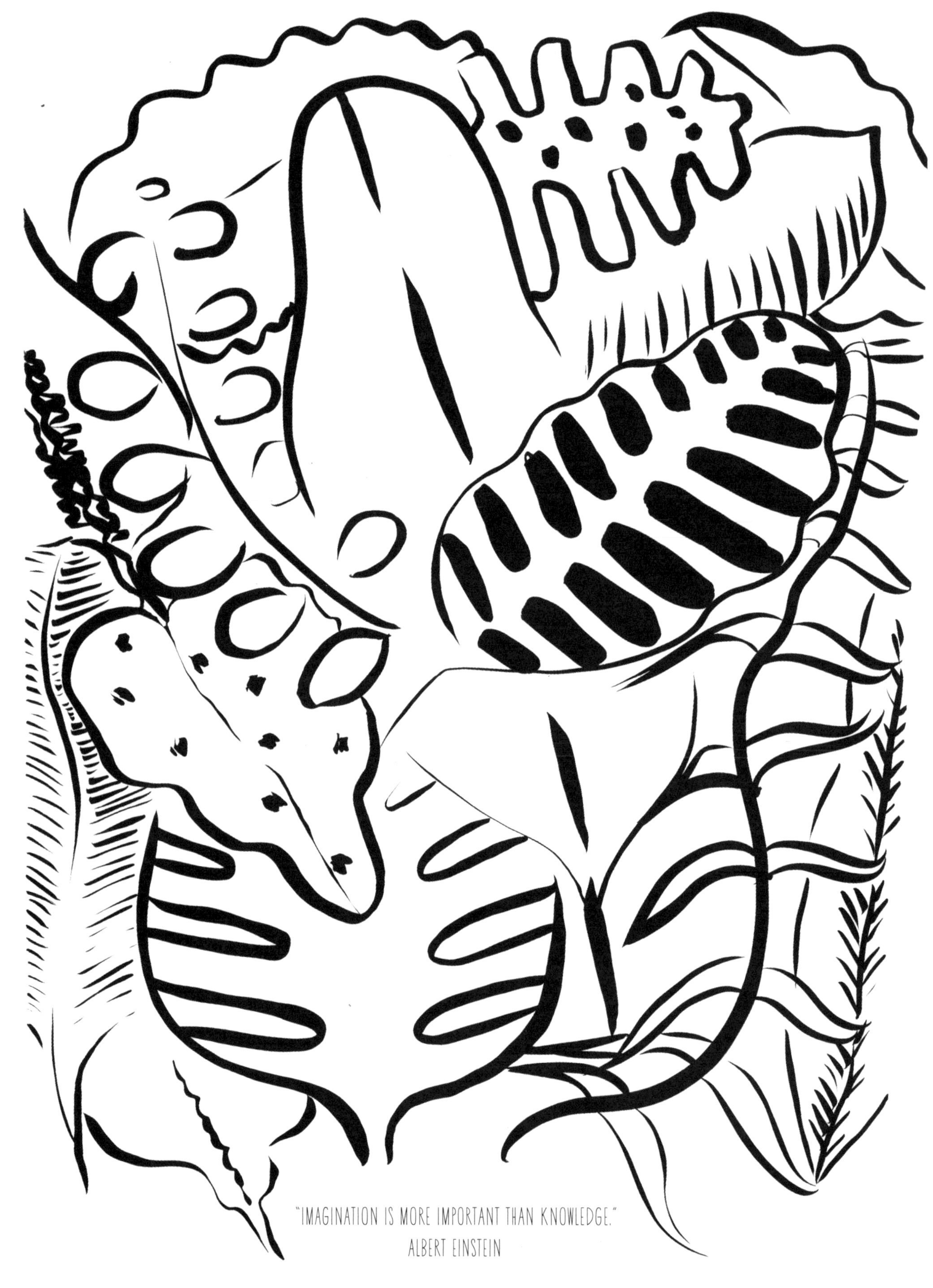

"IMAGINATION IS MORE IMPORTANT THAN KNOWLEDGE."
ALBERT EINSTEIN

CONTENTS

"THE MOST POTENT MUSE OF ALL IS OUR OWN INNER CHILD." STEPHEN NACHMANOVITCH

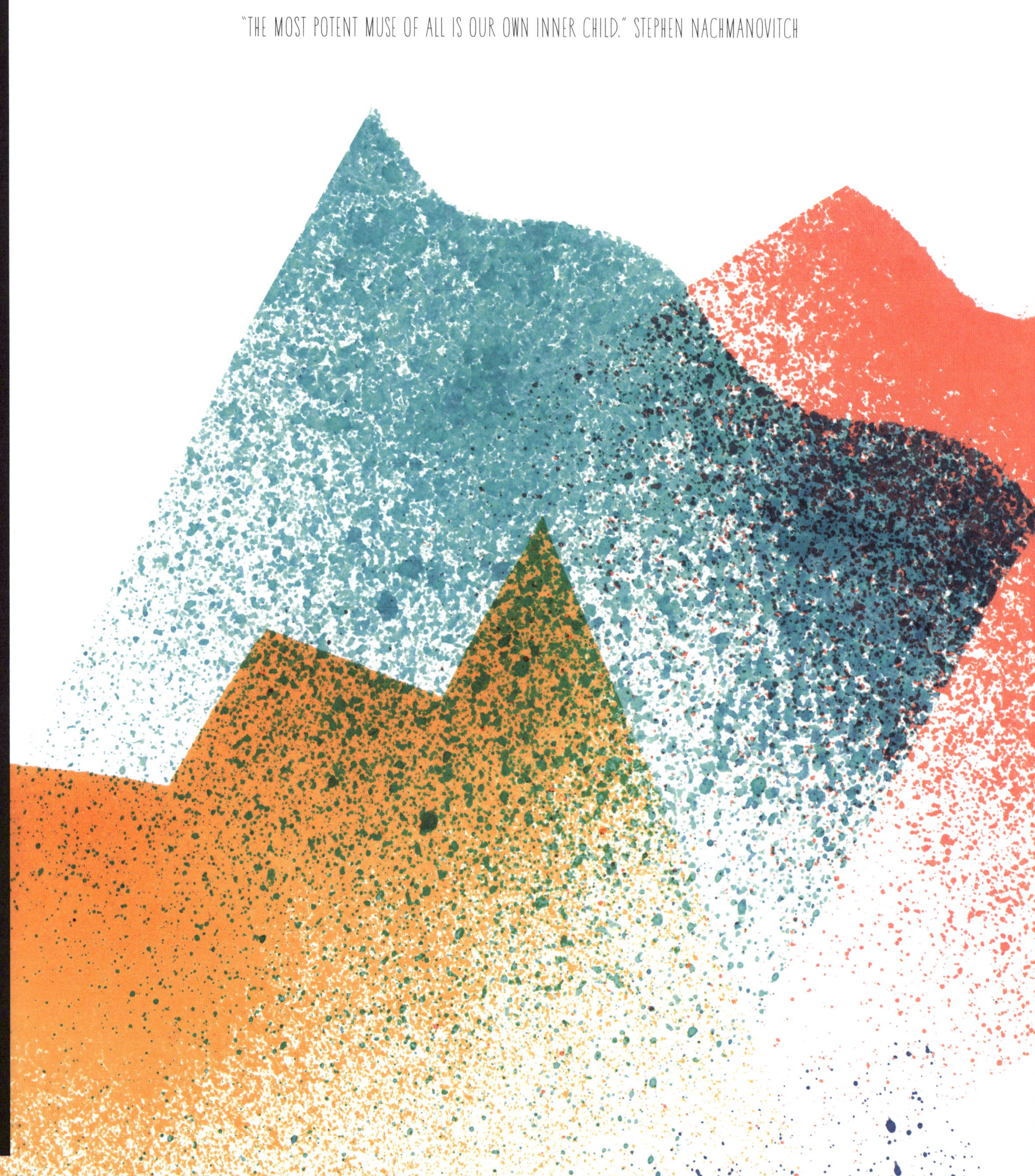

Thank you for choosing this book. I'm very happy to have you here.

Inside this playbook, you'll find exercises that are intended to work as explorations in various pen and ink techniques. I provide instructions and tips, but feel free to experiment in different ways and follow your intuition. The key is to have fun with our inks, pens, and brushes!

The artwork doesn't have to look great all the time, nor does it have to be too detailed or representational. What matters is enjoying the creative process and taking incremental steps toward a more colorful life. Creativity has to be free and never is to be judged. Everything has a place in this world, even the things you consider ugly may seem beautiful to another person!

Experimenting with pen and ink can help you focus on the present moment and allow you to tap into your inner wisdom to find some insight. For me, it is like meditating. When we turn off our rational brain for a while, we can start getting in touch with our wildly creative subconscious mind. This is one of the powers of art.

Be inspired, play, draw—make a mess if you may—clean and repeat. Forever.

Yours in color and shape,

Ana Montiel

MIXING COLORS

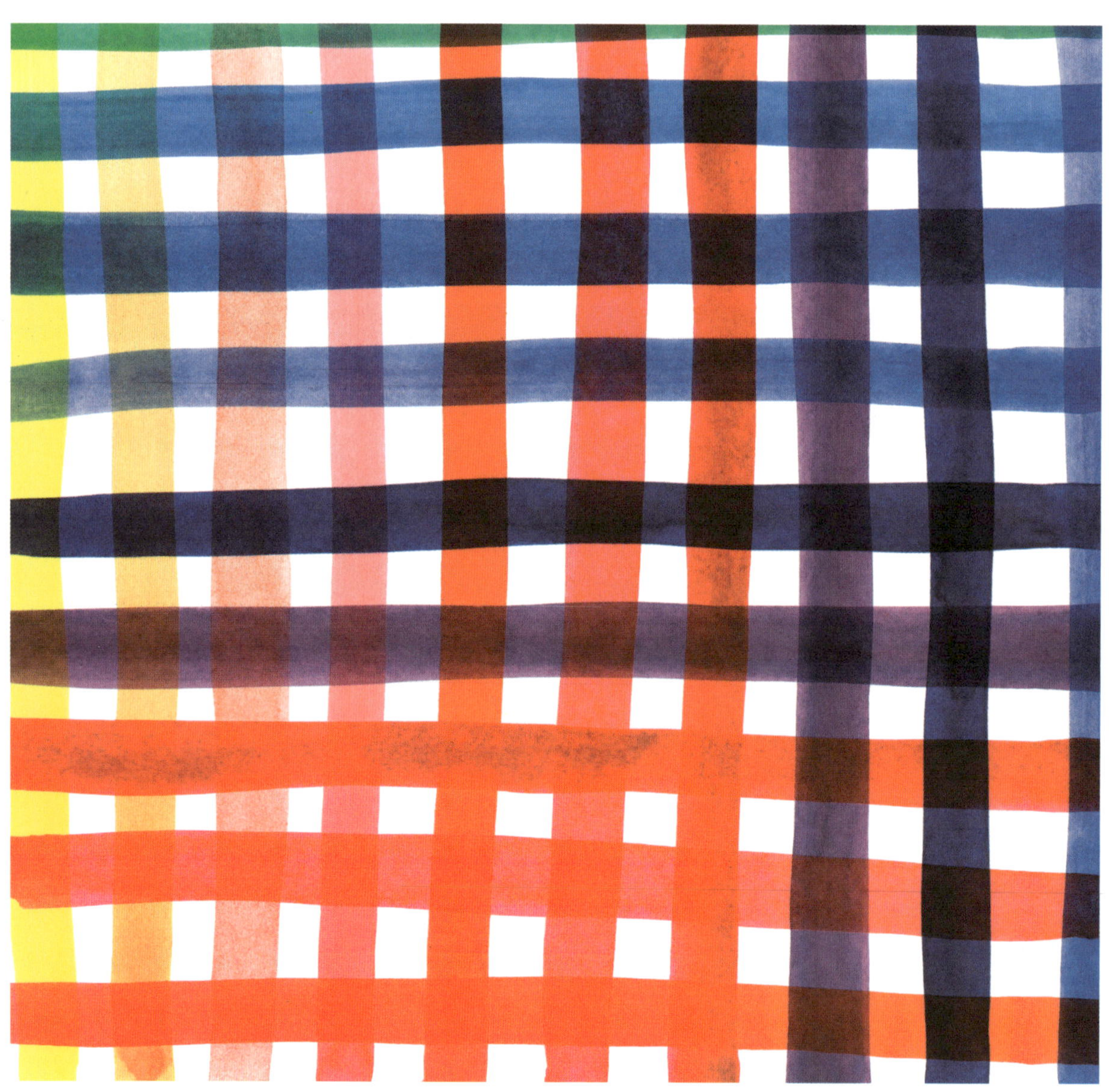

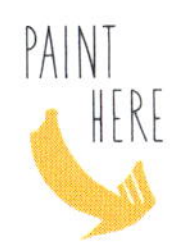

Instead of making the usual color chart, let's try a quicker and easier version. Just make a parallel line of each of the colors that you want to try, let them dry, and cross them with other colors to see how the combination of both hues look when overlapped. Any paintbrush will work here, but for even, straight lines, use a flat brush.

TIP: START WITH LIGHTER COLORS AND CONTINUE WITH DARKER SHADES; THAT WAY, YOU WON'T HAVE TO CHANGE THE WATER THAT OFTEN WHEN CLEANING THE BRUSH BETWEEN COLORS.

PAINTING WITH NATURE

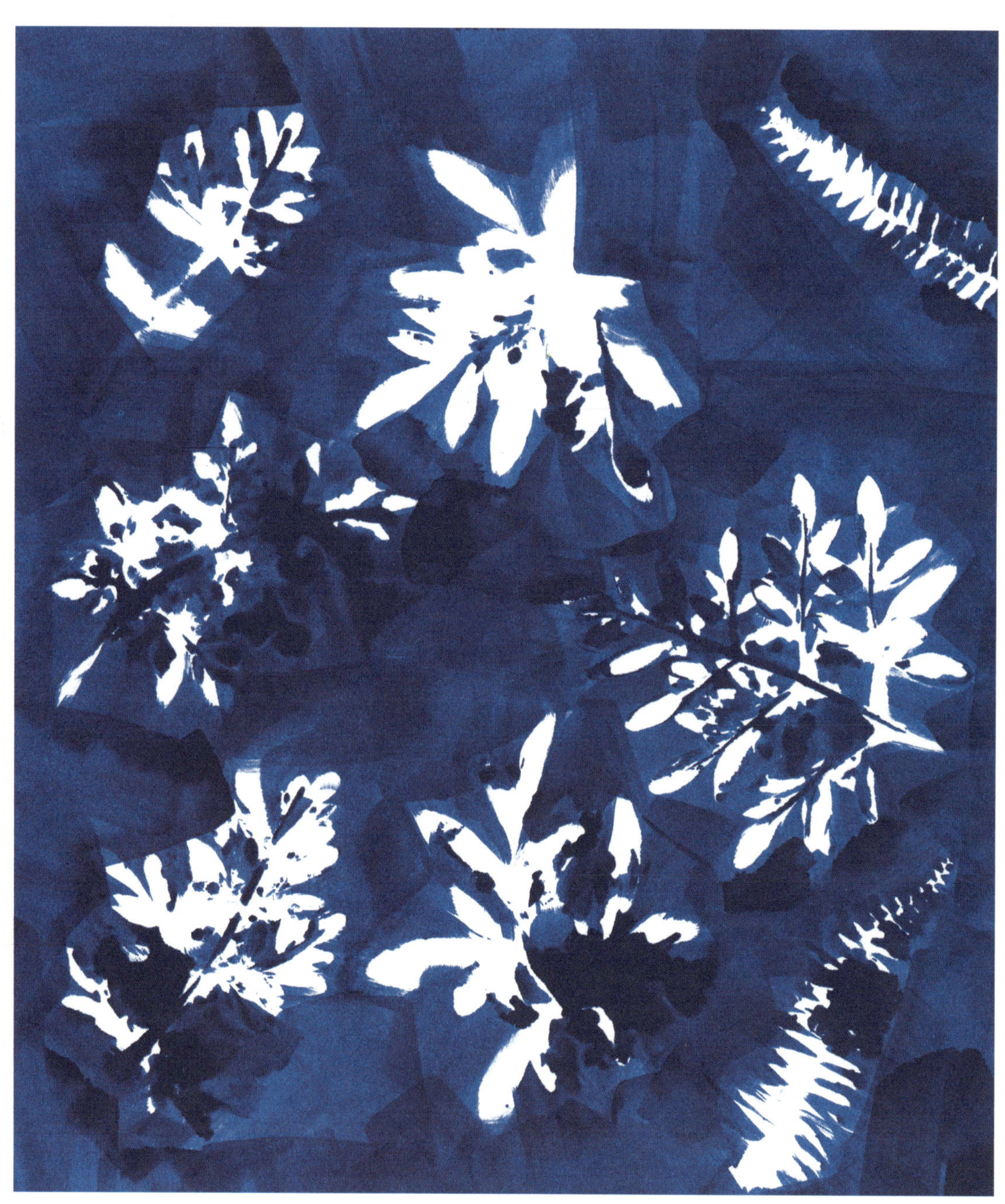

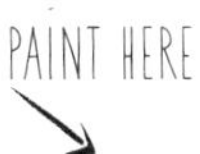

A cyanotype is a photographic blueprint that can be done by placing objects directly on top of photosensitive paper. It was often used to capture the silhouettes of botanical specimens. This exercise has a cyanotype vibe but is created with ink. Go for a walk in nature and select some plant leaves with interesting shapes. Take them home and place them above. Now carefully secure them to the paper with your fingers, and apply ink around them with a brush—center of the leaf to its edges—to capture their silhouettes.

TIP: YOU CAN USE A PAIR OF TWEEZERS OR SOMETHING SIMILAR TO SECURE THE LEAVES TO THE PAPER IF THEY ARE TOO SMALL TO ANCHOR WITH YOUR FINGERS.

DESIGN A RUG

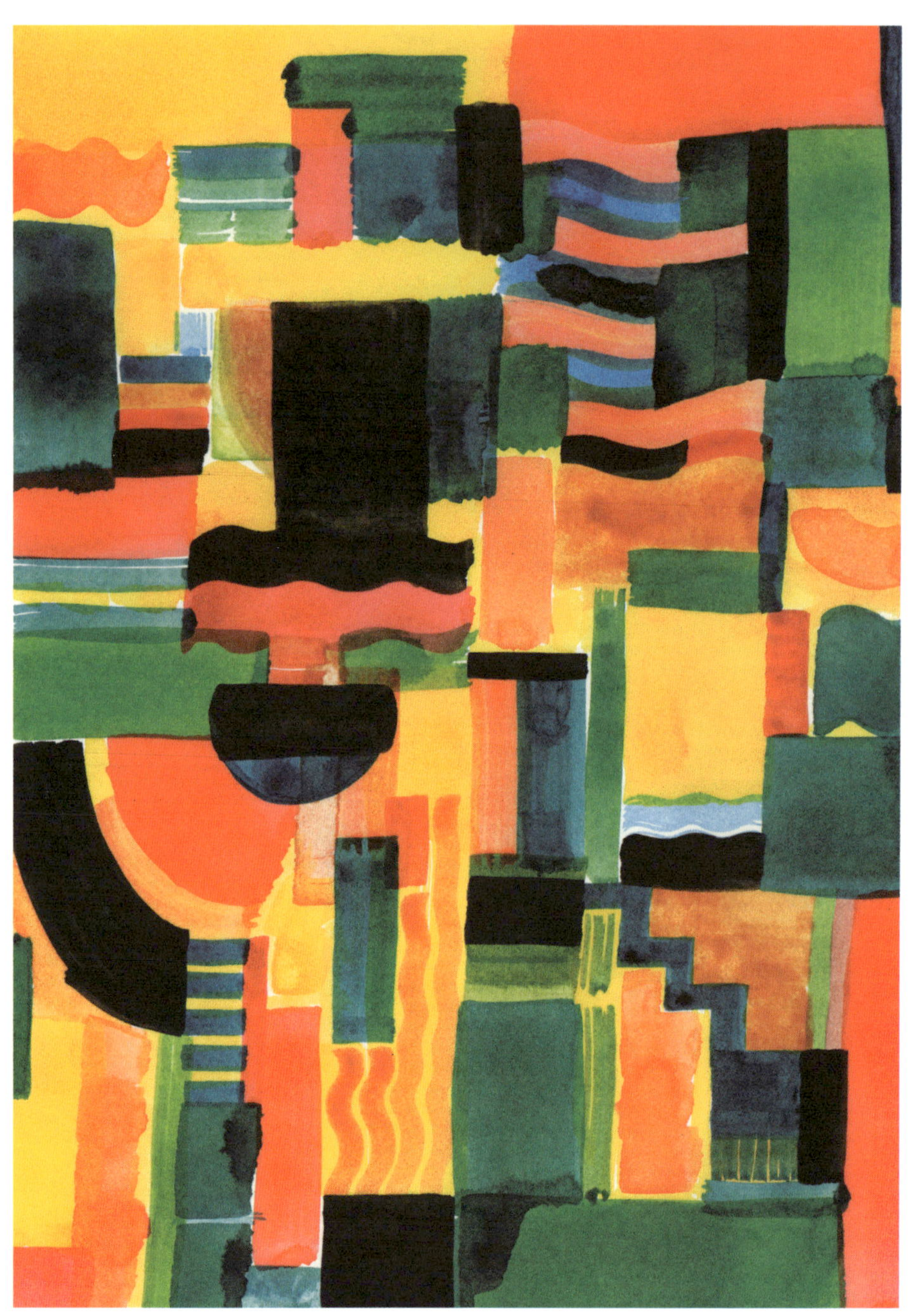

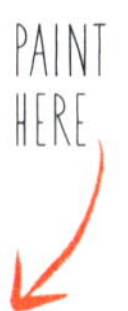

Imagine a rug that you'd love to have in your place. Is it minimalistic in design? Is it monochromatic? Is it super bold? Now design your own rug on this page. Outline its shape—it doesn't have to be rectangular—play with the composition, and have fun with your brushes. For inspiration, search online for Moroccan, Bauhaus, or Oaxacan rugs.

TIP: FOR THE EXAMPLE ON THE OPPOSITE PAGE, I WORKED WITH WATER-BASED INKS THAT I MIXED MYSELF. START BY APPLYING LIGHTER HUES AND THEN ADD DARK VALUES TO CREATE CONTRAST AND BALANCE.

SALAD SPINNER

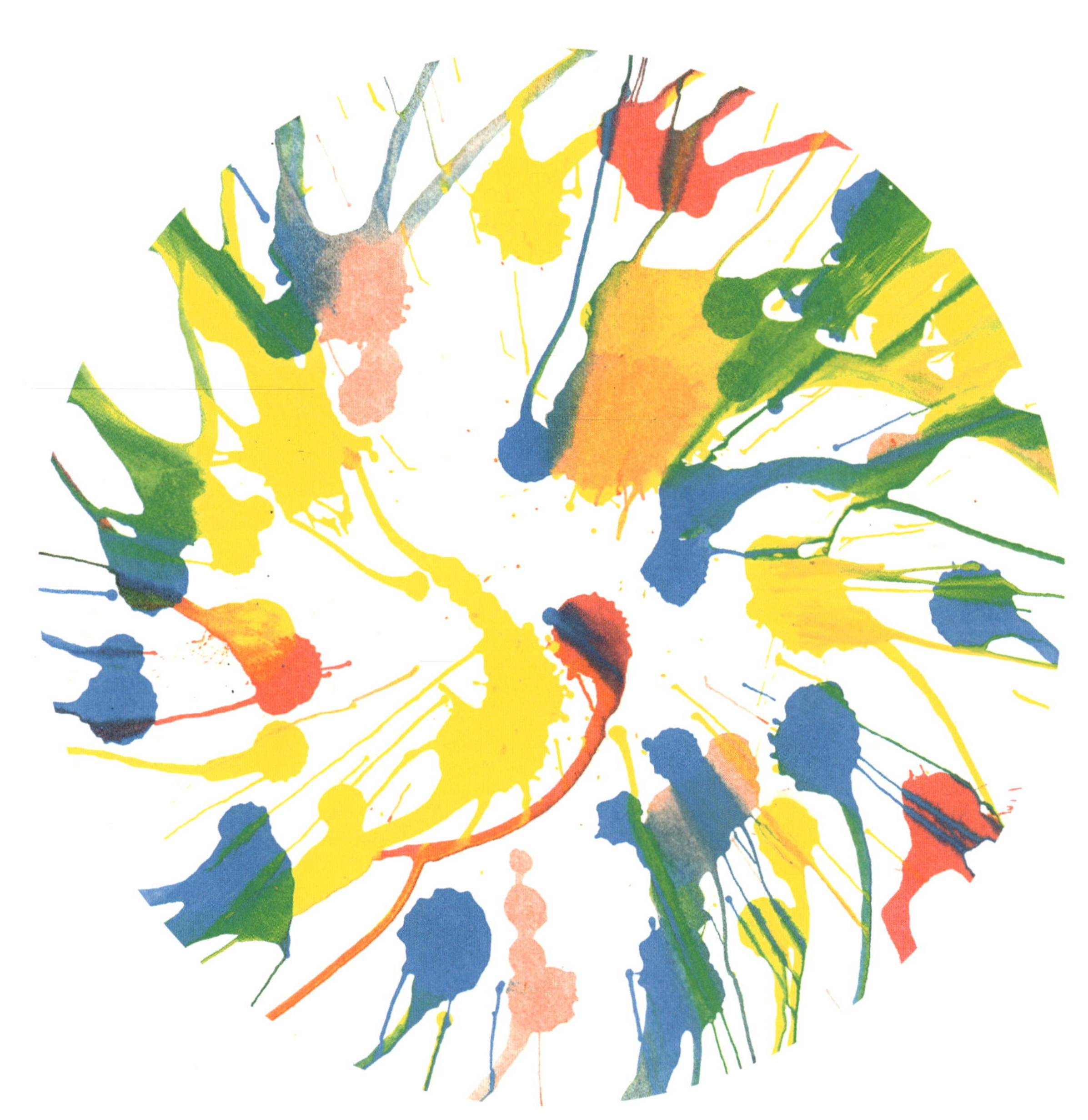

If you have a toddler nearby, do this exercise with him or her. If you don't, invite your inner child to the party because it is a fun one! Cut a sheet of paper to fit the inside of a salad spinner. Place it in the spinner, quickly drop water-based ink on top of it, close the lid, and spin it as fast as you can. After 10 or 15 seconds, take the lid off and see your psychedelic painting!

TIP: ALCOHOL-BASED INKS WILL PERMANENTLY STAIN THE SPINNER. INSTEAD, USE WATER-BASED INKS AND CLEAN THE SPINNER WITH WARM WATER AND SOAP IMMEDIATELY AFTER USING IT.

MOTH PATTERNS

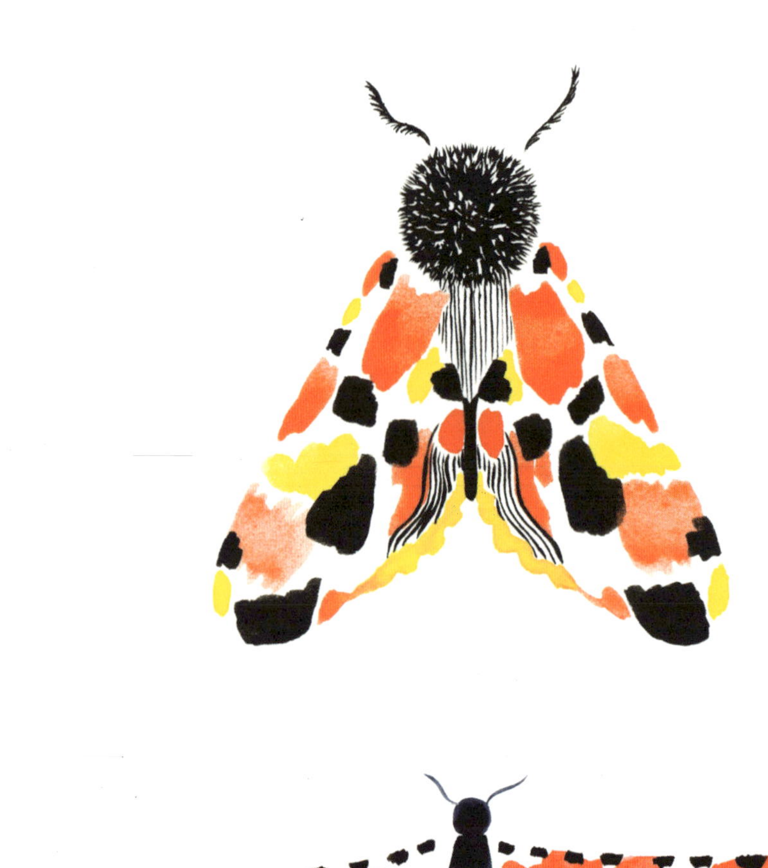

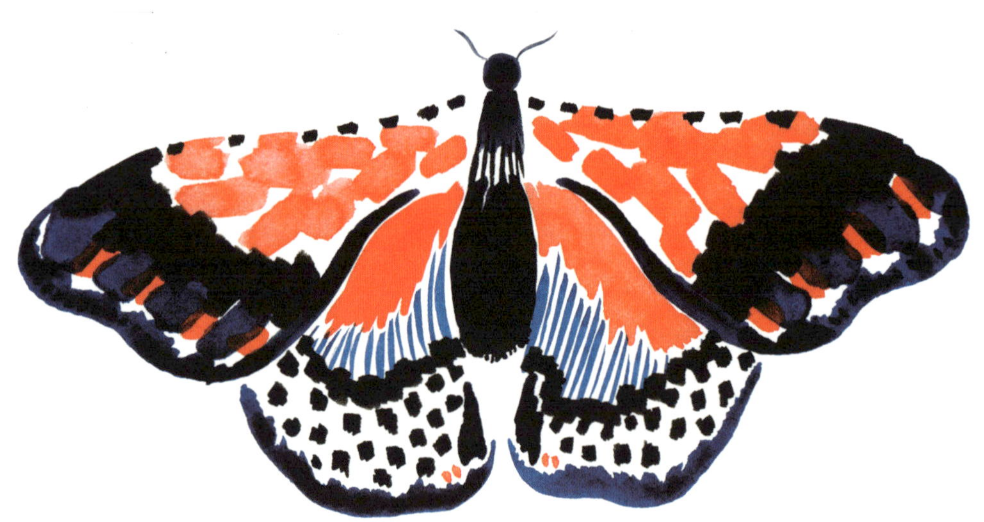

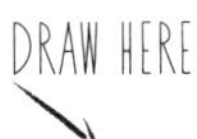

Moths have the most amazing patterns. Make up a couple of new species for this exercise. First outline on cardstock or similar paper the left or right section of a moth you like. Cut its shape and trace its contour with a pencil above this text. Now flip the stencil and trace its mirrored image. Ready to go wild with pattern? Three, two, one—go!

TIP: MAKE YOUR PATTERN OR DESIGNS AS SYMMETRICAL AS POSSIBLE ON THE LEFT AND RIGHT SET OF WINGS. THAT WILL GIVE YOUR PAINTINGS MORE MOTH CREDIBILITY. YOU CAN USE PENS TO ADD THE DETAILS!

DIP DIP

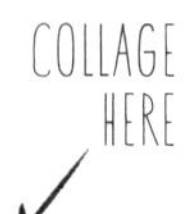

Sometimes no brush is the best brush. Make a shallow pool of ink (add water to lighten it) and dip the centers of several strips of paper into it. Start with lighter hues. Let them dry. When dry, dip them again in a different hue to see how the colors overlap. Cut the pieces and arrange them above in a collage, or work with larger paper to better appreciate your pieces. They will look great framed!

TIP: I DID THIS EXERCISE WITH WATER-BASED INKS AND PAPER, BUT YOU CAN TRY IT WITH FABRIC AND ALCOHOL-BASED INKS (WEAR GLOVES, PLEASE). THIS TECHNIQUE WOULD BE PERFECT FOR MAKING A BOHEMIAN-CHIC SCARF.

OPAQUE WHITE SPLATTER

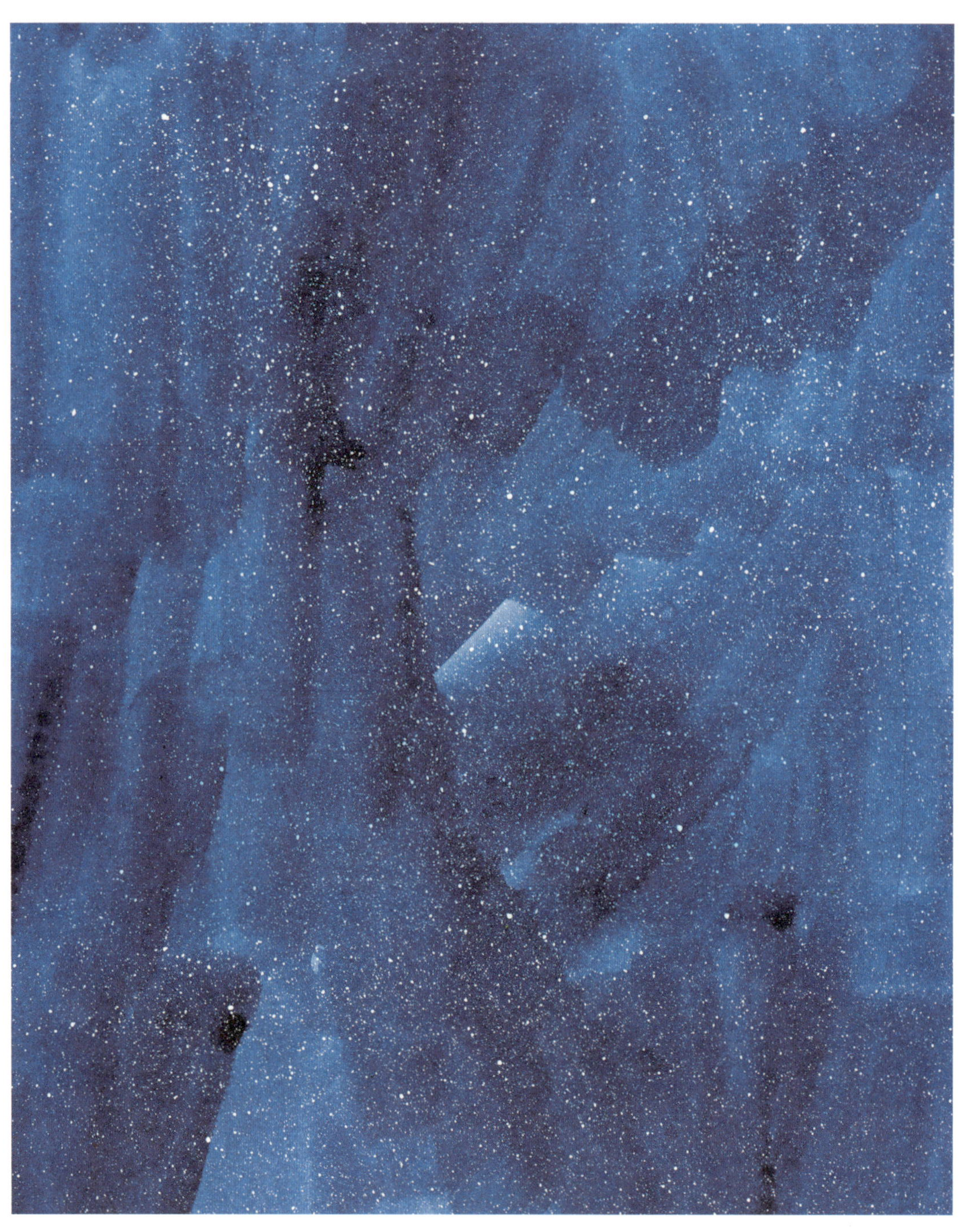

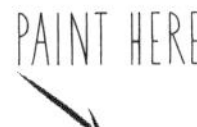

Load a thick soft brush with ink. Cover the drawing area completely with it, allowing irregularities on the surface to enrich the painting. When the color background is dry, dip an old toothbrush in white paint, hold it over the paper with the bristles facing down, and slide your finger along the bristles to release the splatter. Play with the distance and angle between the toothbrush and the paper for splatter variations.

TIP: IT'S VERY IMPORTANT TO APPLY THE SPLATTER WITH OPAQUE INK IF YOUR BACKGROUND IS DARK AND THE SPLATTER IS LIGHTER. USE ACRYLIC INKS BECAUSE THEY HAVE A THICKER, MORE OPAQUE FINISH.

NEGATIVE SPACE

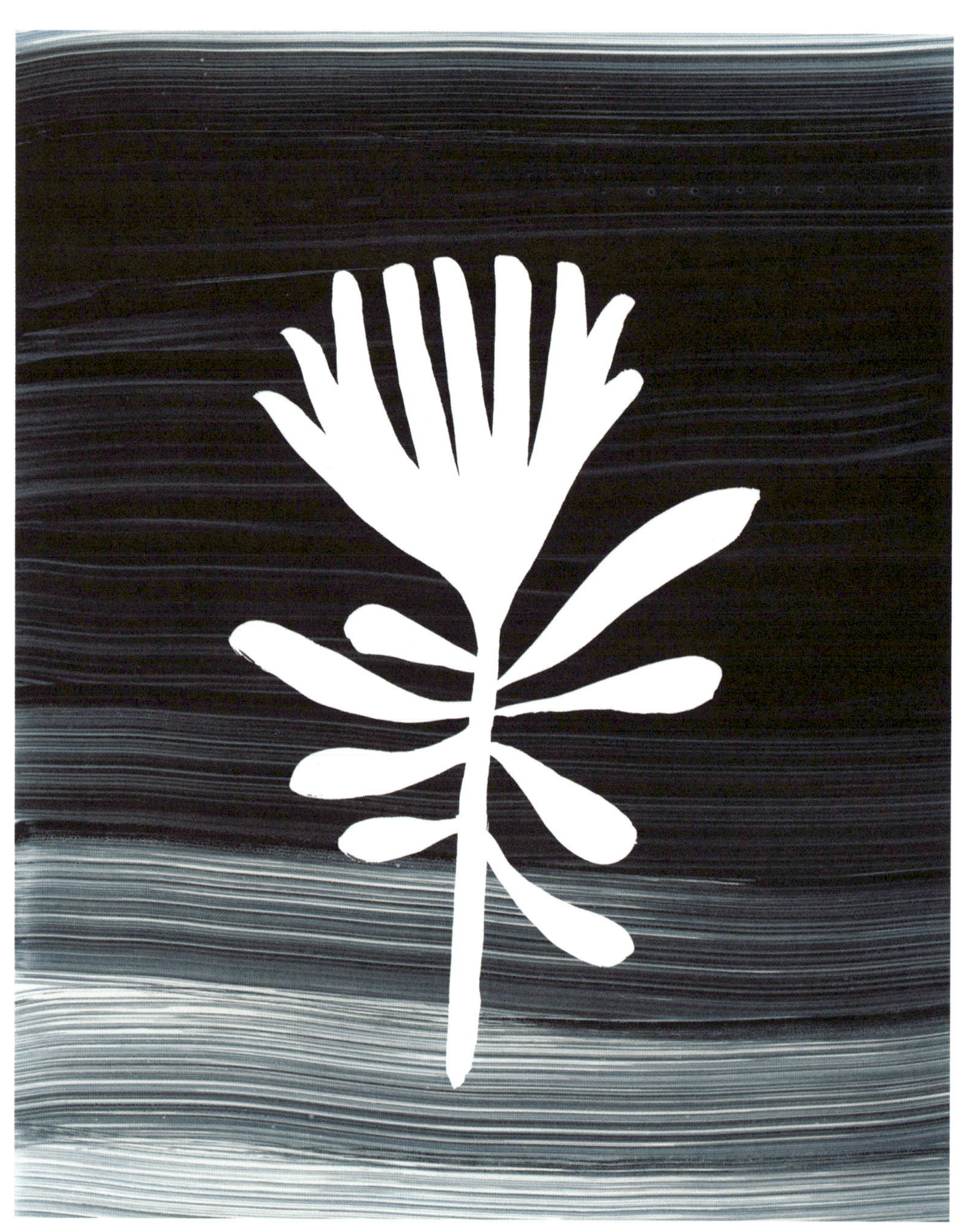

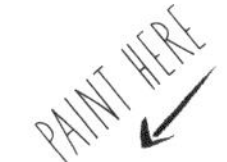

Frisket is a masking fluid or adhesive paper typically used in watercolor painting to cover areas on the paper the artist doesn't want painted—it's great for painting with ink, too. Draw the outline of your painting above with pencil, apply frisket on top of it, and let it dry. Color around it to create a background and notice the motif appearing in the noncolored space. When dry, remove the frisket and the pencil outline with a soft eraser.

TIP: GET FRISKET THAT IS WHITE OR TRANSPARENT BECAUSE THE COLORED ONES CAN SOMETIMES TINT THE PAPER. TO APPLY THE FRISKET, USE AN OLD, CHEAP BRUSH THAT YOU DON'T MIND GETTING COMPACTED AND SLIGHTLY DAMAGED.

DROPPER BOMBS

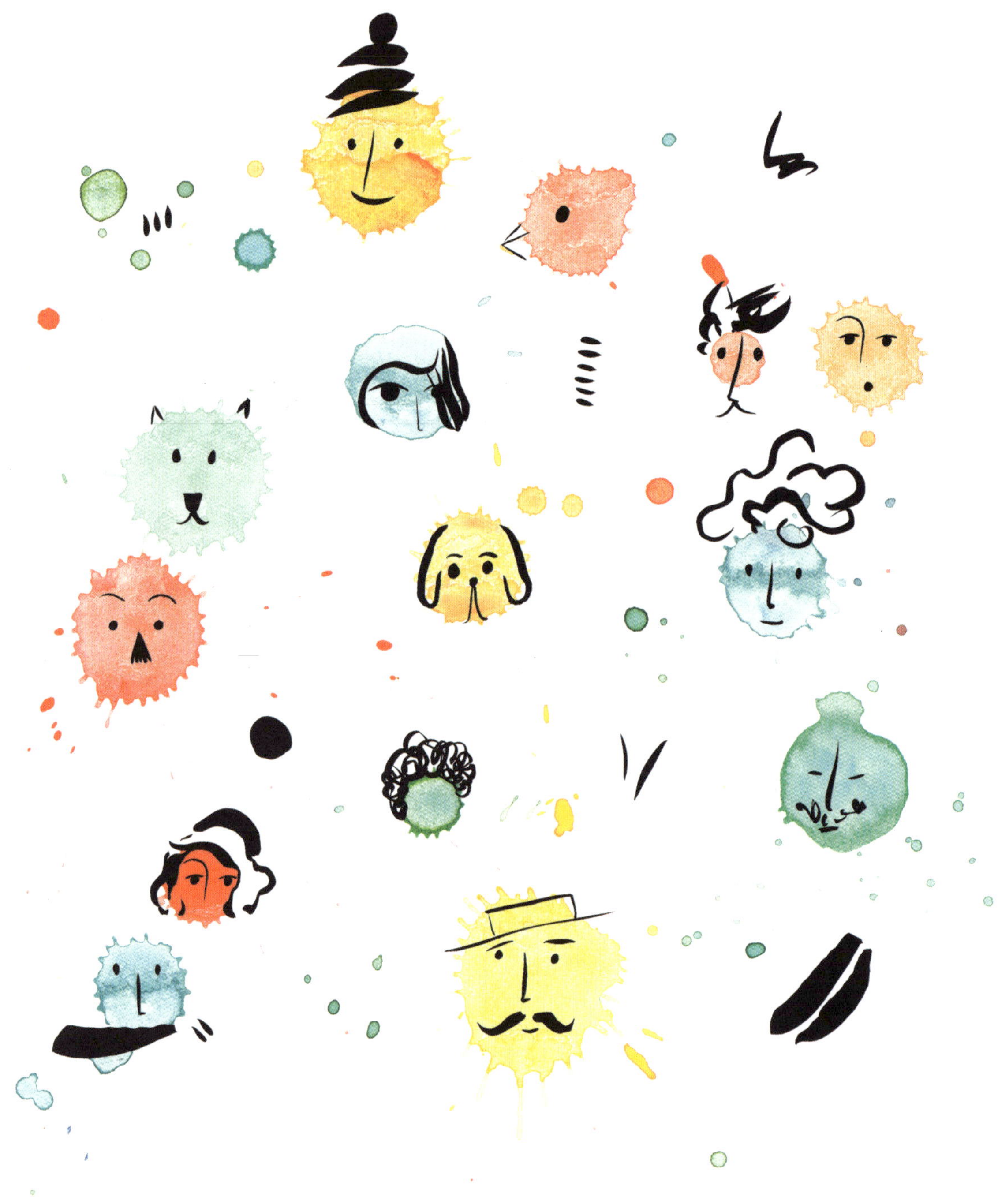

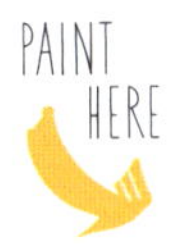

Any shape in the world can be turned into a character. For example, we could see faces in a lot of places and objects if we pay attention. Experiment and make some random shapes by dropping ink onto the paper. When the ink is dry, paint some facial features on each. Think of different personalities for each of them and sketch them accordingly.

TIP: THE FEATURES CAN BE VERY ABSTRACT. IF THE SHAPE CONTAINS SOMETHING SIMILAR TO AN EYE, FOR EXAMPLE, DRAW A NOSE AND MOUTH BELOW IT. TO MAKE THE SHAPES, USE A BRUSH OR DROPPER LOADED WITH INK.

SALT TEXTURE

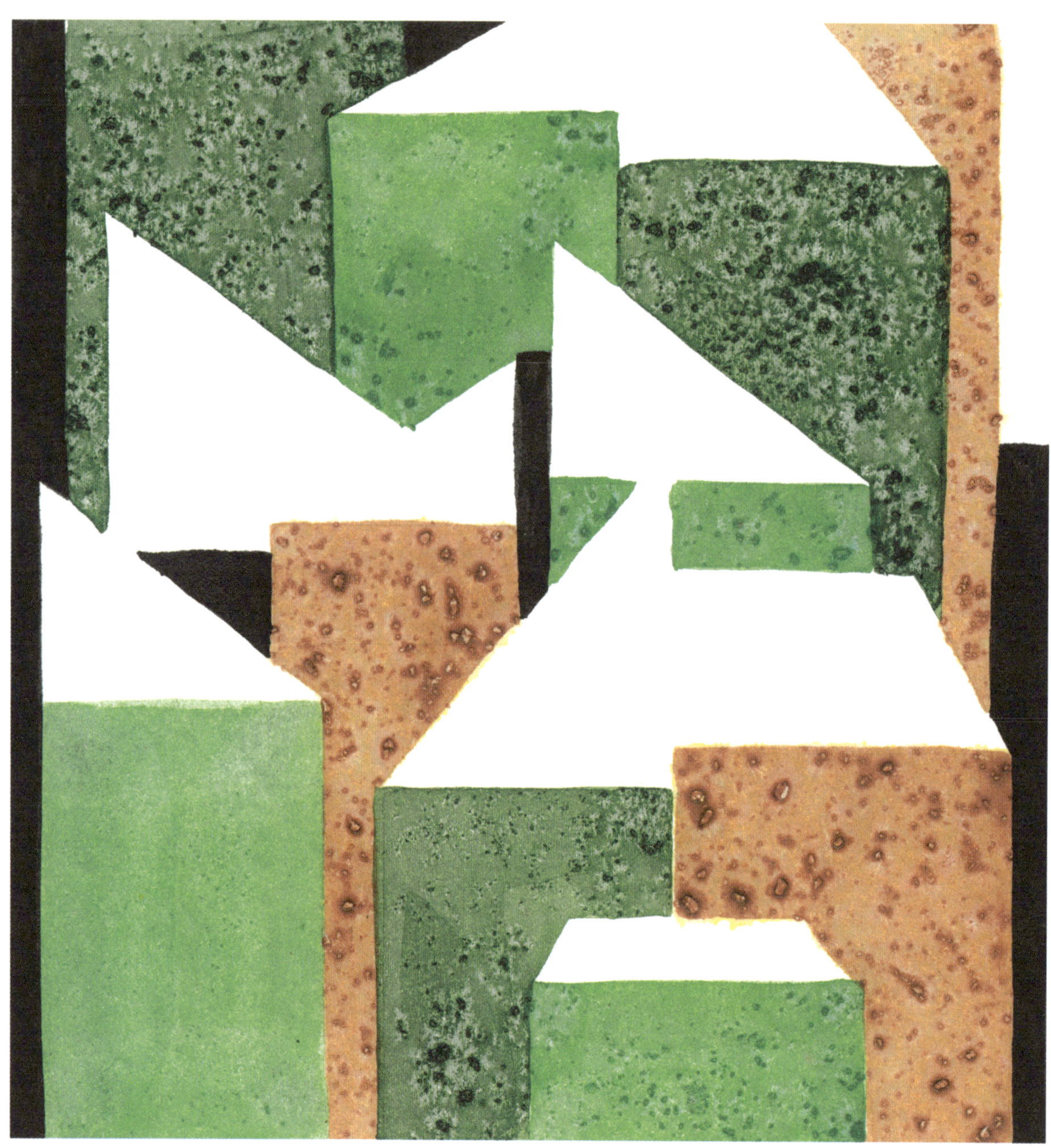

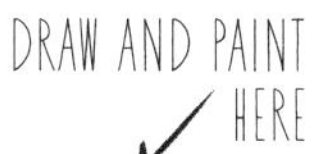

For this exercise, we'll play with salt to achieve more complex textures on our ink surfaces. To start, outline your painting design above with a pencil and start applying color with your inks and a brush. Sprinkle some salt on top of the ink while it's still wet. Let it dry and then remove the tiny salt particles left on the painting with a brush or your hand.

TIP: TO CREATE A DIFFERENT TEXTURE, DROP SOME GRAINS OF RICE ON TOP OF THE INK WHILE IT'S STILL WET. THE RICE WILL ABSORB SOME OF THE INK, CREATING LIGHTER AREAS IN YOUR PAINTING.

KEEPING PROPORTIONS

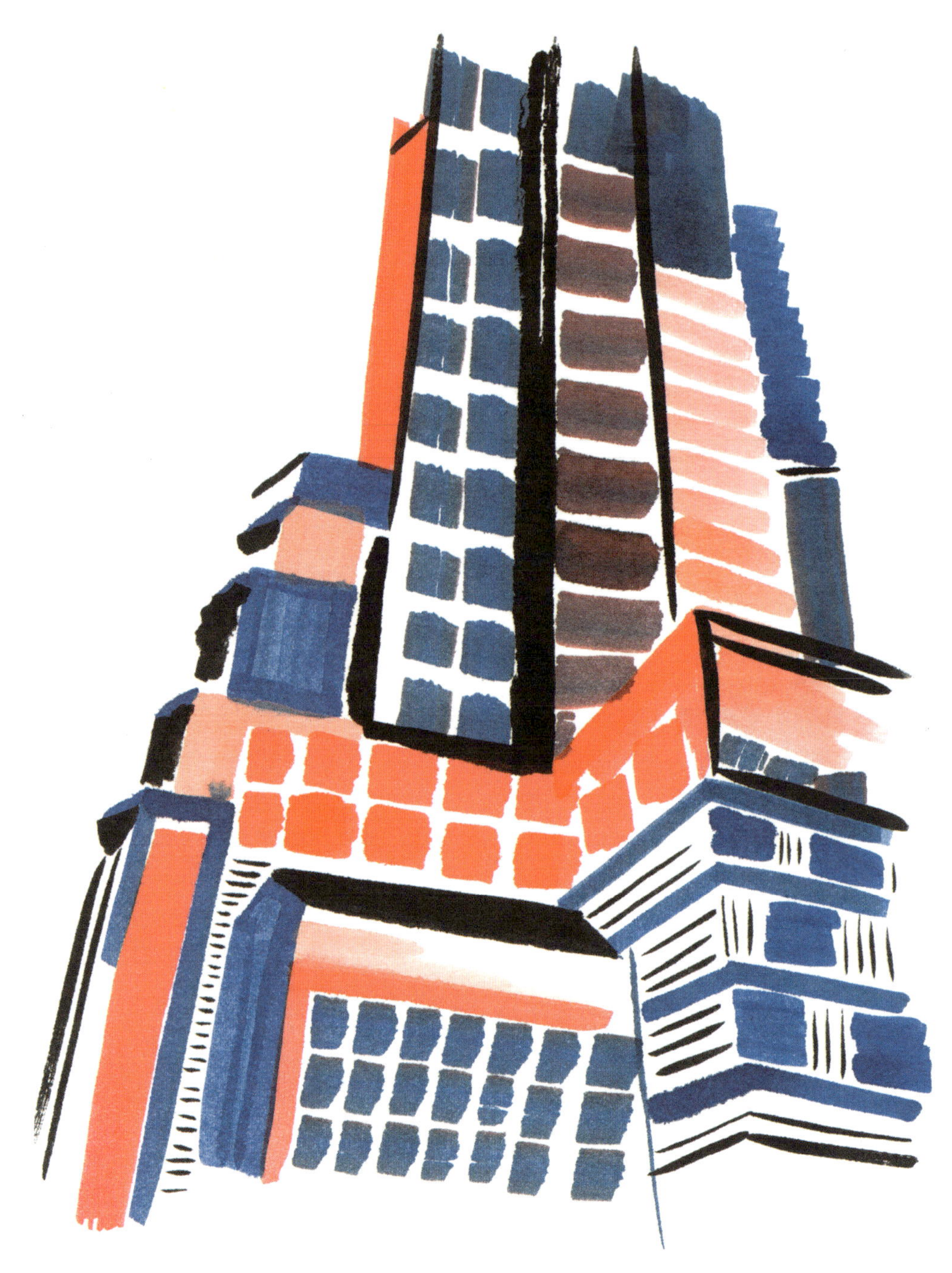

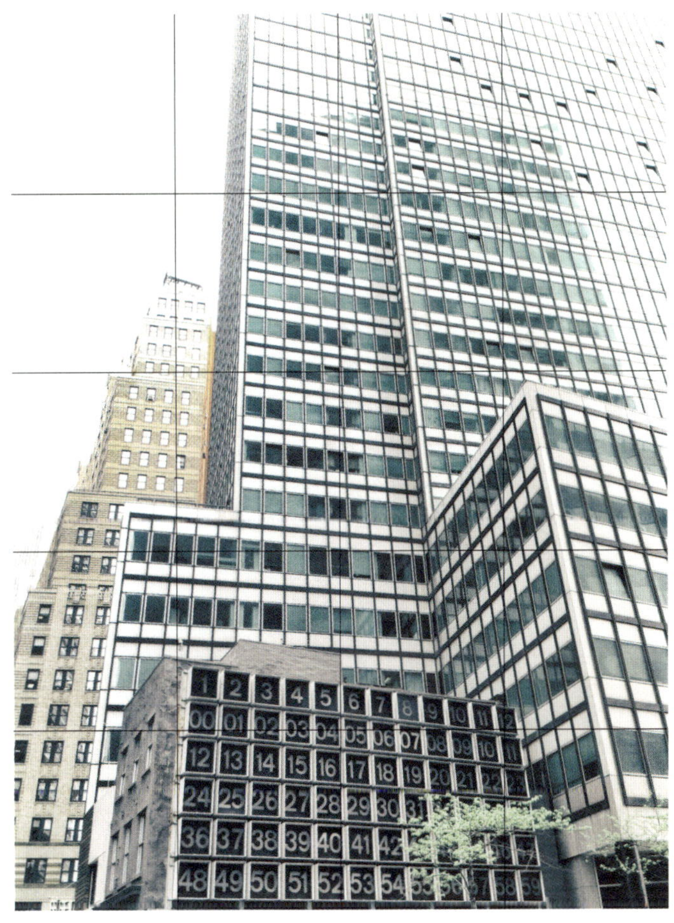

A grid is immensely helpful to keep proportions as accurate as possible when painting and sketching. Take a picture of something that you want to turn into a painting. Print it out and draw a grid on top of it. Draw another grid with the same measurements on the paper you'll be painting. When sketching, notice the elements in your photo in relation to the edges and areas of the grid. For example, is the end of the element in the middle or at the edge of the square?

TIP: FIRST SKETCH YOUR PICTURE WITH A PENCIL, ERASE THE GRID WHEN DONE, AND THEN APPLY COLOR WITH INKS. THIS WAY, YOU'LL HAVE A CLEANER PAINTING WITHOUT THE PENCIL GRID MARKS.

MODULAR PATTERN

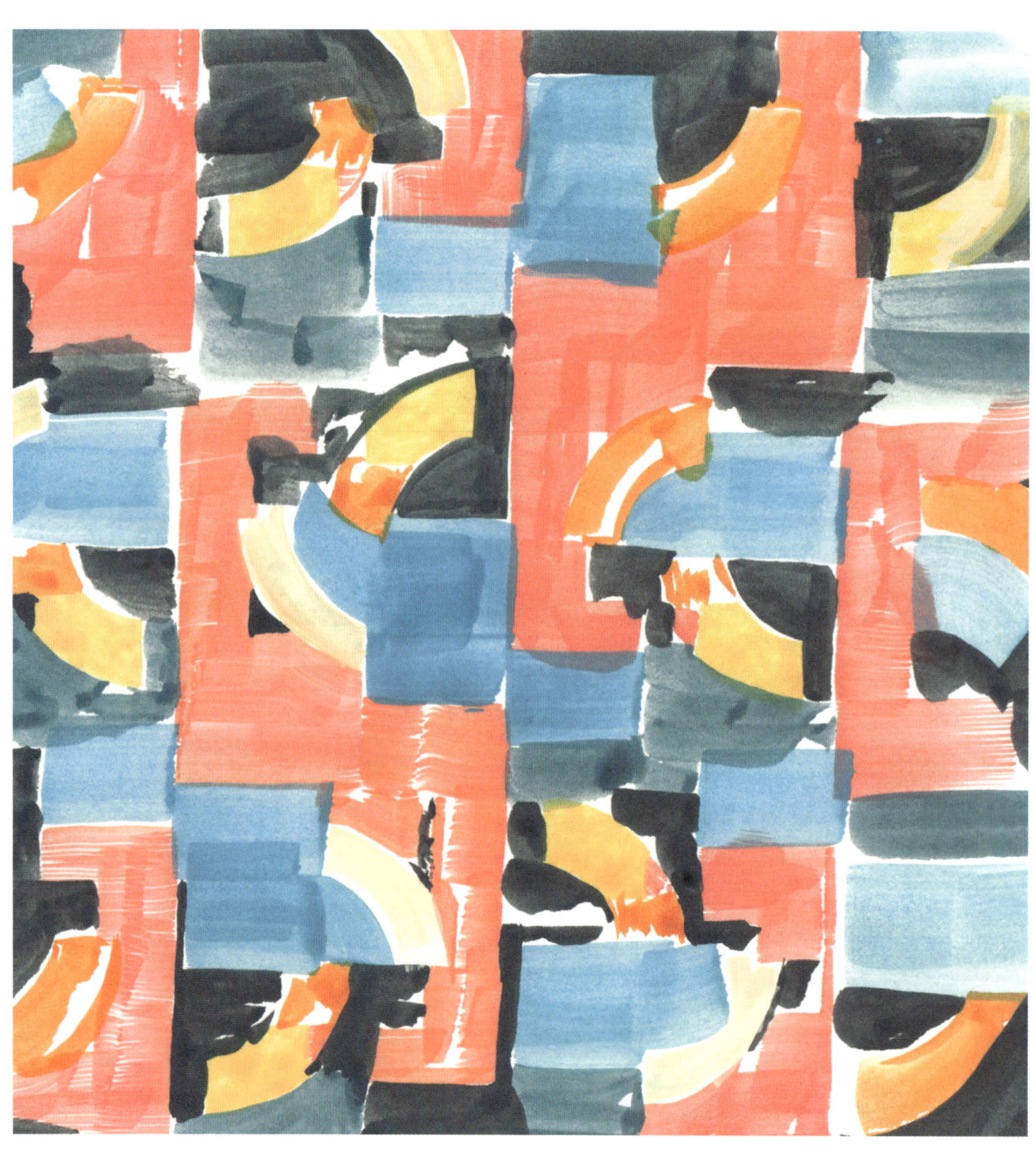

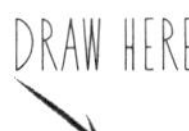

To create a modular pattern like the one opposite, draw the repeat piece on a sheet of paper. It can be anything you want. Using carbon paper, trace the repeat piece many times above, side by side to create the pattern structure. Use light-colored carbon paper for the outlines so they disappear when covered with color afterward.

TIP: EXPERIMENT WITH SUBTLE, MORE COMPLEX COLORS ON YOUR PALETTE BY ADDING A BIT OF BLACK AND/OR WHITE TO YOUR MIXES. WHITE WILL MAKE THEM LOOK A BIT PASTEL-LIKE AND BLACK WILL MUTE THEM SLIGHTLY.

POSITIVE NEGATIVE

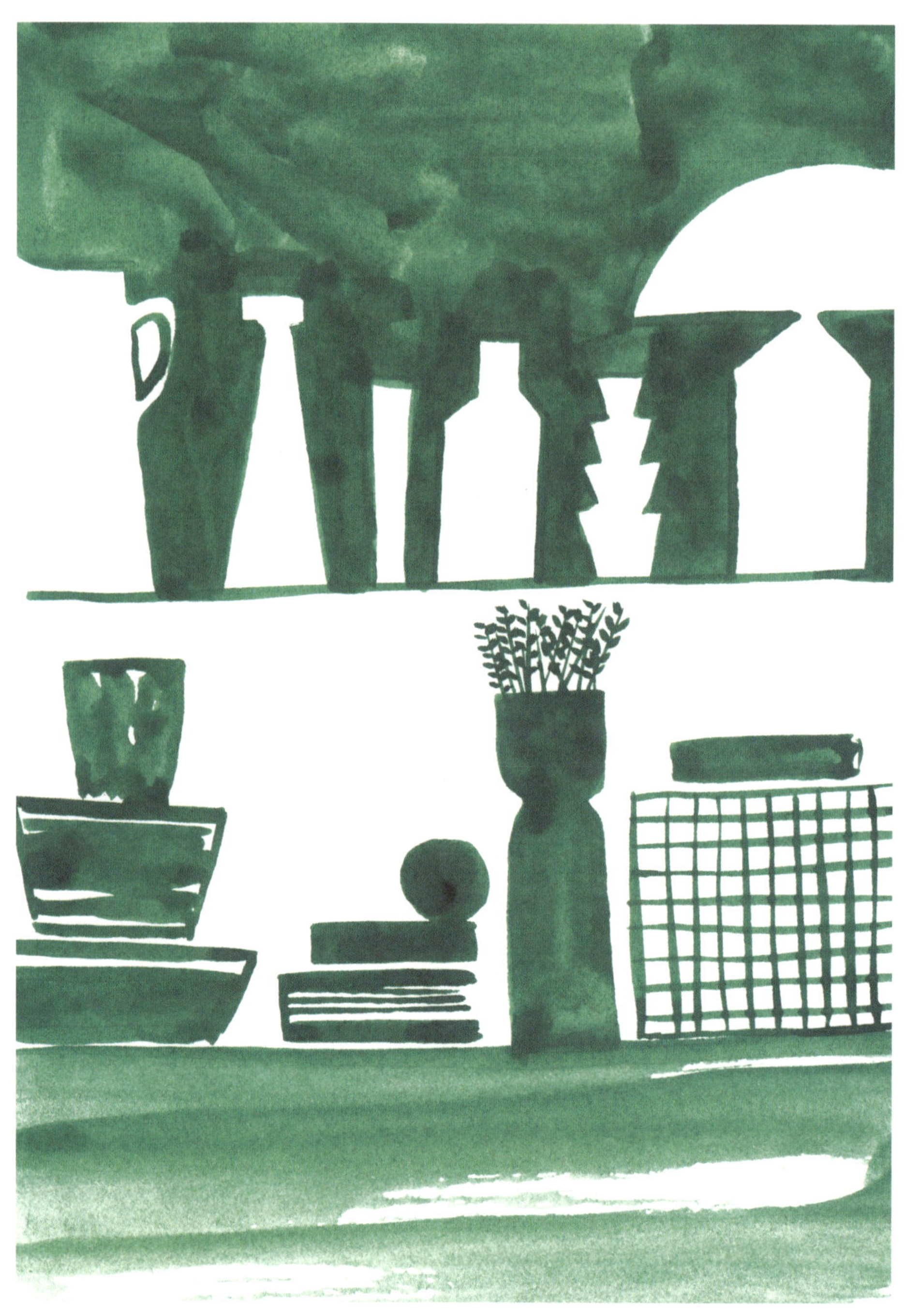

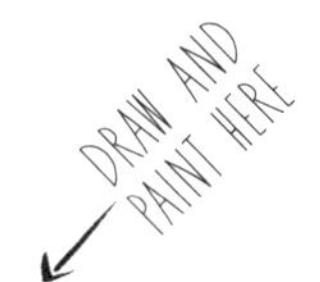

Choose a color for your painting. Find a subject with two very defined parts. Sketch the composition with a pencil and paint one of its halves, leaving the main figures in white and coloring just the background. For the other half, color the objects and leave the background white. Play with contrast and textures to enrich your artwork.

TIP: A STILL LIFE WOULD BE IDEAL FOR THIS EXERCISE. ARRANGE SOME OBJECTS YOU LIKE AND USE TWO DIFFERENT BACKGROUNDS; THE BACKGROUND DIVISION WILL DEFINE THE COLOR INVERSION.

FREESTYLE STENCIL

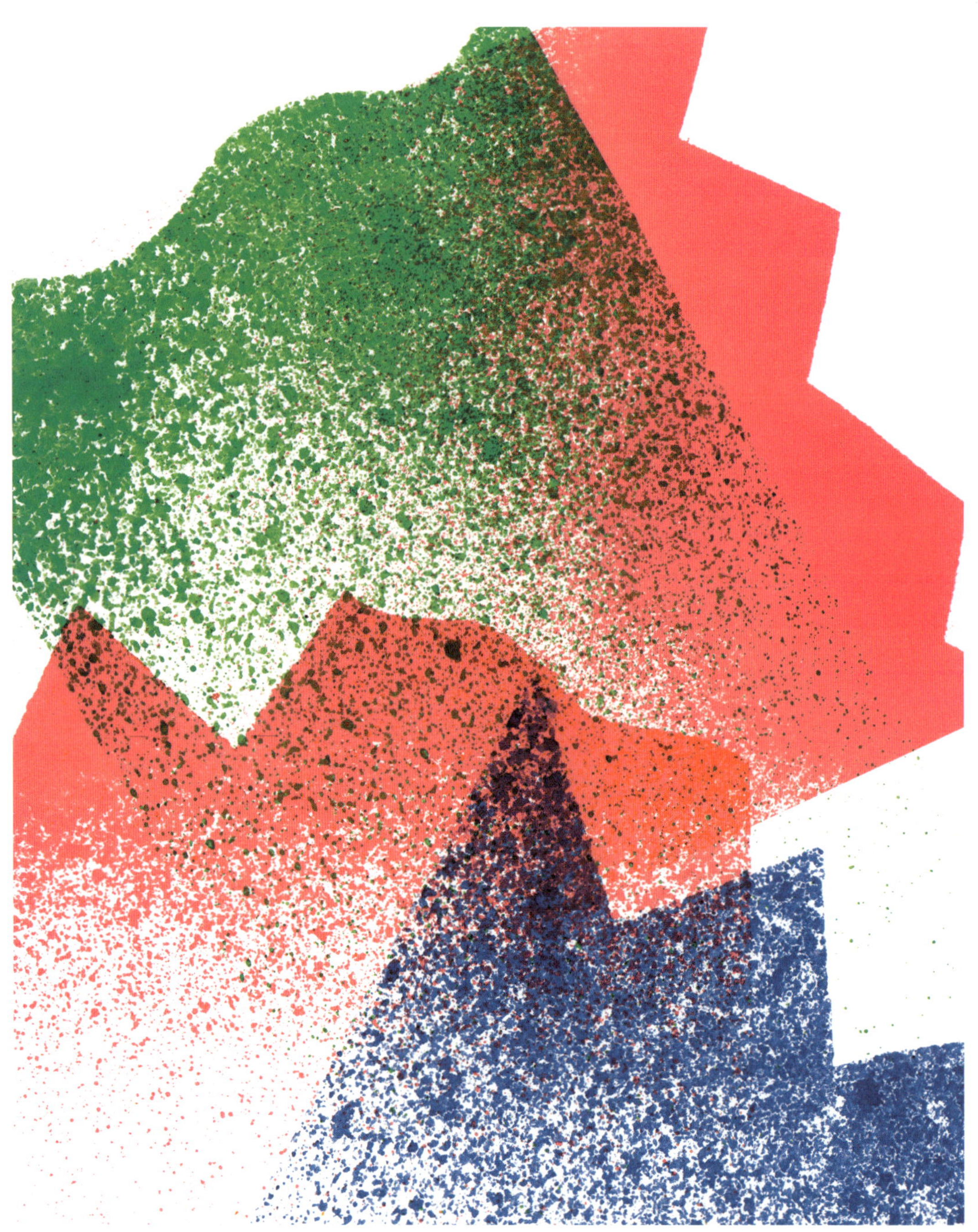

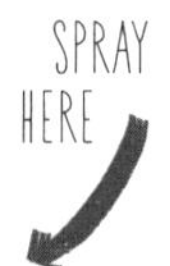

For this exercise, I used alcohol-based inks, but you can use water-based ones if you want. Add a small amount of ink to a tiny spray bottle and spray it above or over a piece of paper partially covered by a stencil, a piece of cardboard, or plastic. Let it dry. Now cover another area. Spray a different color on top of the previous layer. Continue to build color as much as you want! Don't forget to protect your work area from unwanted ink splatter, especially if you are working with alcohol-based inks.

TIP: IF USING A SINGLE SPRAY BOTTLE, START WITH THE LIGHTEST HUE. WHEN EMPTY, ADD THE NEXT SLIGHTLY DARKER HUE TO THE BOTTLE AND CONTINUE WITH YOUR PAINTING. REPEAT WITH EACH HUE AND HAVE FUN!

PLAYING WITH FRISKET

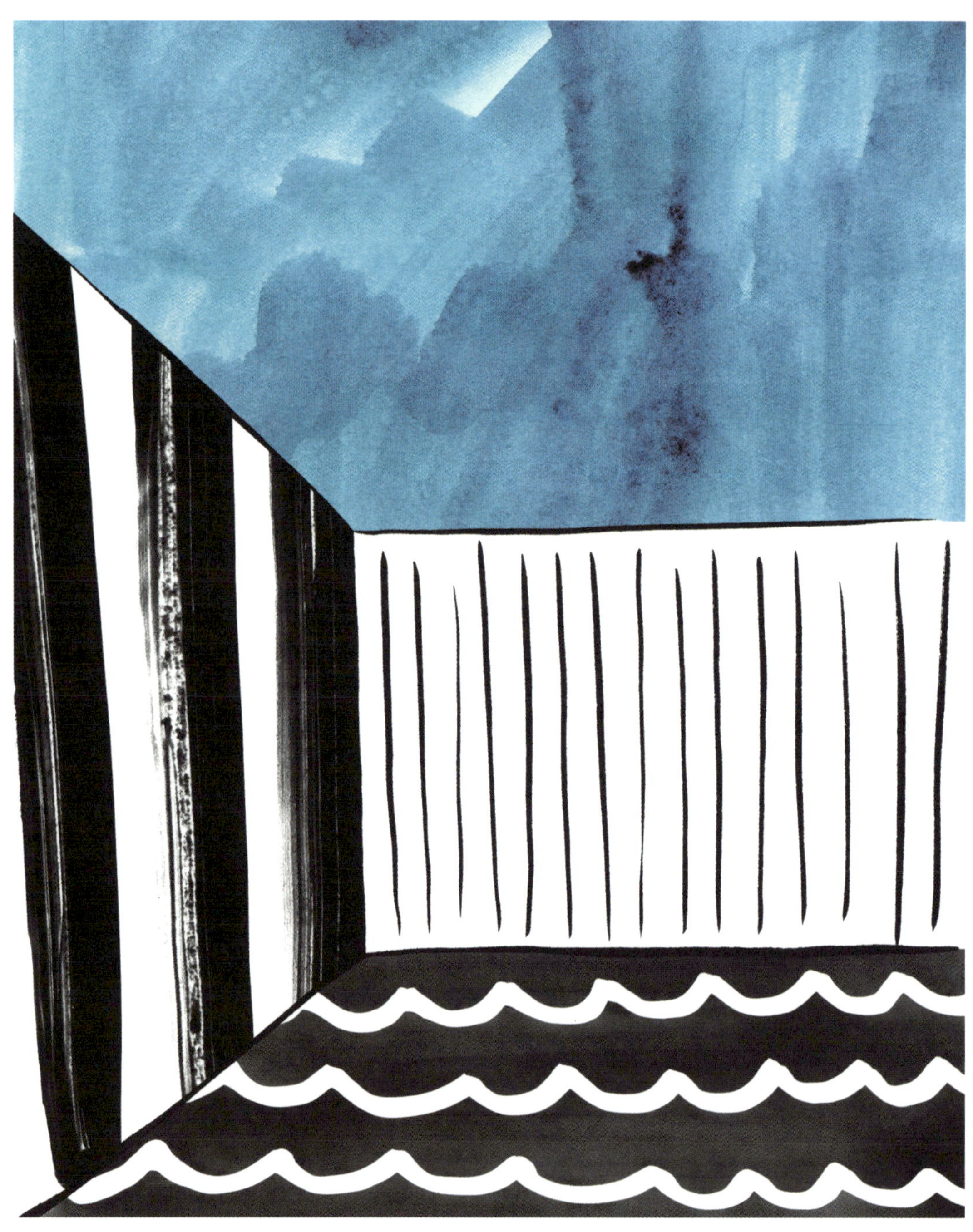

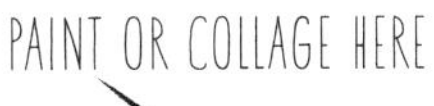

You can achieve simple graphic lines or textures with color and white space by outlining your painting with a pencil and then choosing the areas in which you want your textures to be white. Apply frisket on them to mask the white areas—see frisket tips on page 21. Let it dry, color, and continue with the rest of your painting. Paint solid washes, add details and textures with different hues, and remove the frisket when done.

TIP: TURN THIS EXERCISE INTO A COLLAGE: APPLY FRISKET AND INK ON DIFFERENT PIECES OF PAPER; CUT, ARRANGE, AND PASTE THEM ABOVE OR ON ANOTHER PIECE OF PAPER; AND FINISH PAINTING ON TOP OF THE COMPOSITION.

PROFILES

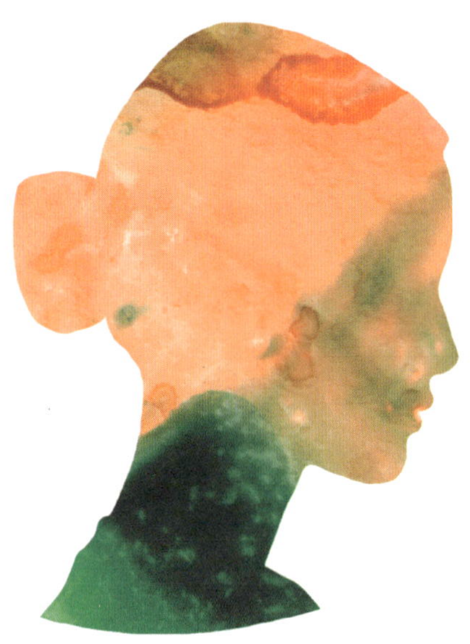

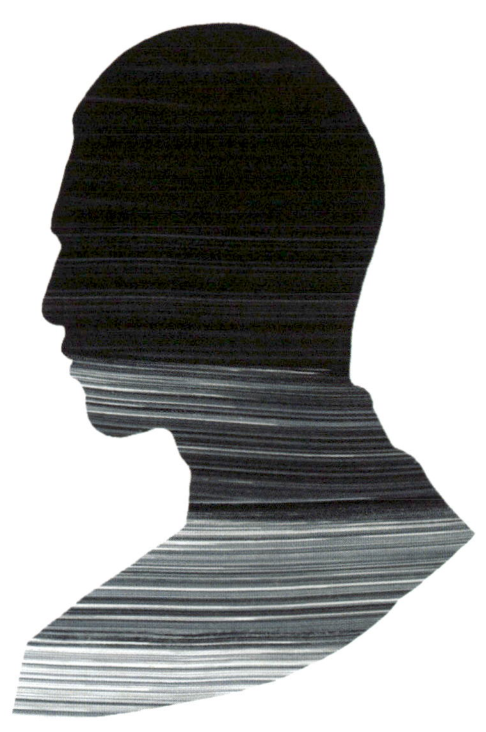

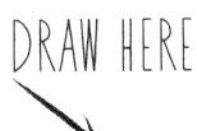

Have a friend stand in front of a light so that you can see his or her silhouette clearly. Start outlining it. If he or she moves too much or distracts you, you can always take a picture of the person and work quietly at another time. When happy with your outline, start coloring. To do this, use any technique and color you prefer.

TIP: YOU DON'T HAVE TO USE A HUMAN SILHOUETTE. START WITH SIMPLER ONES, SUCH AS A LEAF OR CHAIR. YOU CAN ALSO CREATE A STENCIL OUT OF THE SILHOUETTE TO MAKE A SERIES WITH DIFFERENT TECHNIQUES AND RESULTS.

PSYCHEDELIC INKS

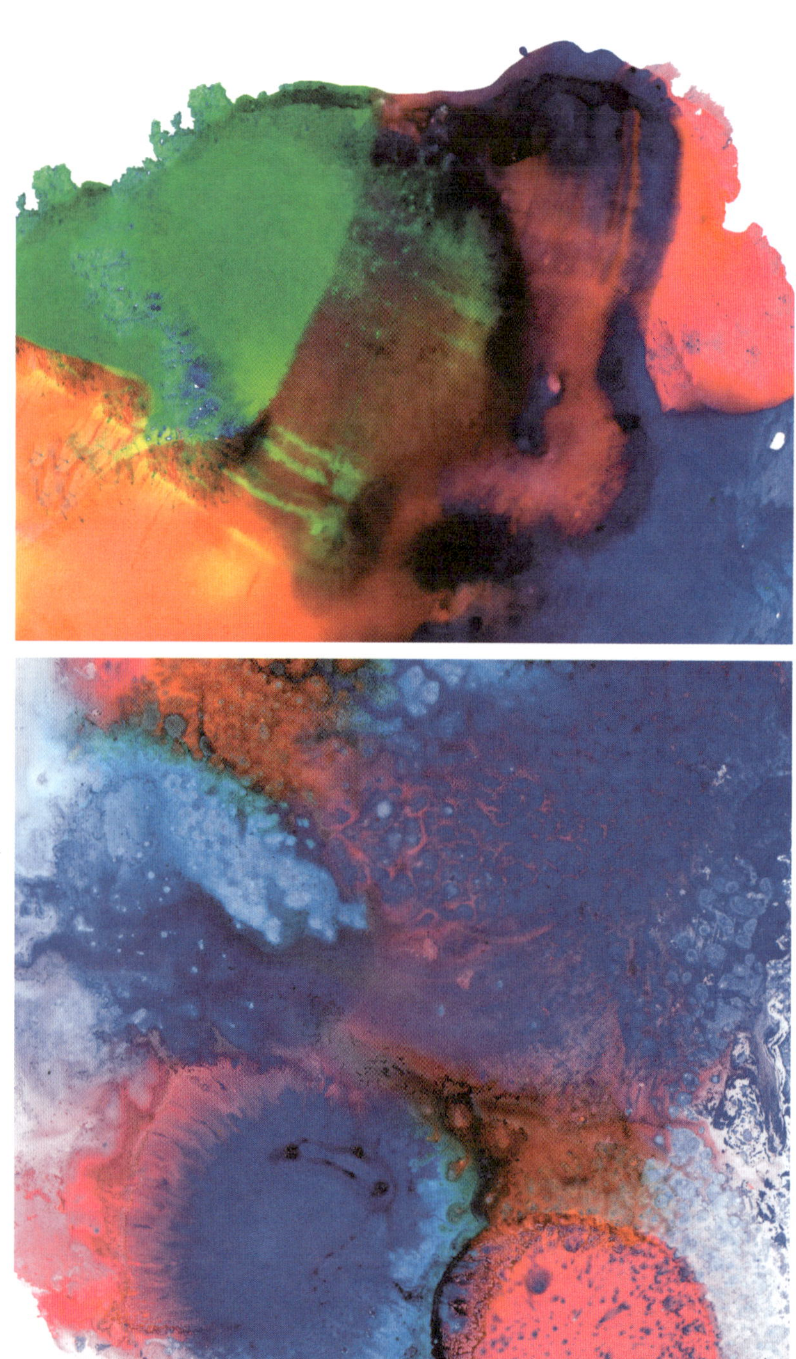

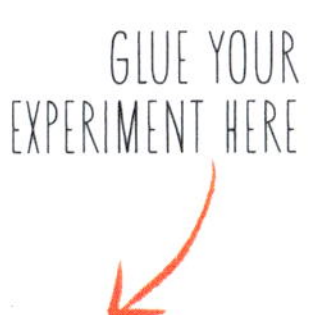

Alcohol-based inks evaporate and get soaked into the paper very quickly. Use synthetic paper such as Yupo or heavyweight coated paper when working with them. You can try many different techniques, but a good way to start is by dropping ink on different areas of the paper and letting it mix. To further mix the ink, add ethanol or blending liquid on top of it. Try a dropper to apply the inks, too. It can give a rich texture to your painting.

TIP: USE LATEX GLOVES OR BE VERY CAREFUL WHEN HANDLING ALCOHOL-BASED INKS. THEY CAN IRRITATE YOUR SKIN! PROTECT YOUR WORK SURFACE WITH PLASTIC, CARDBOARD, OR PAPER TO AVOID DYING YOUR WORKING TABLE.

ANIMAL PORTRAIT

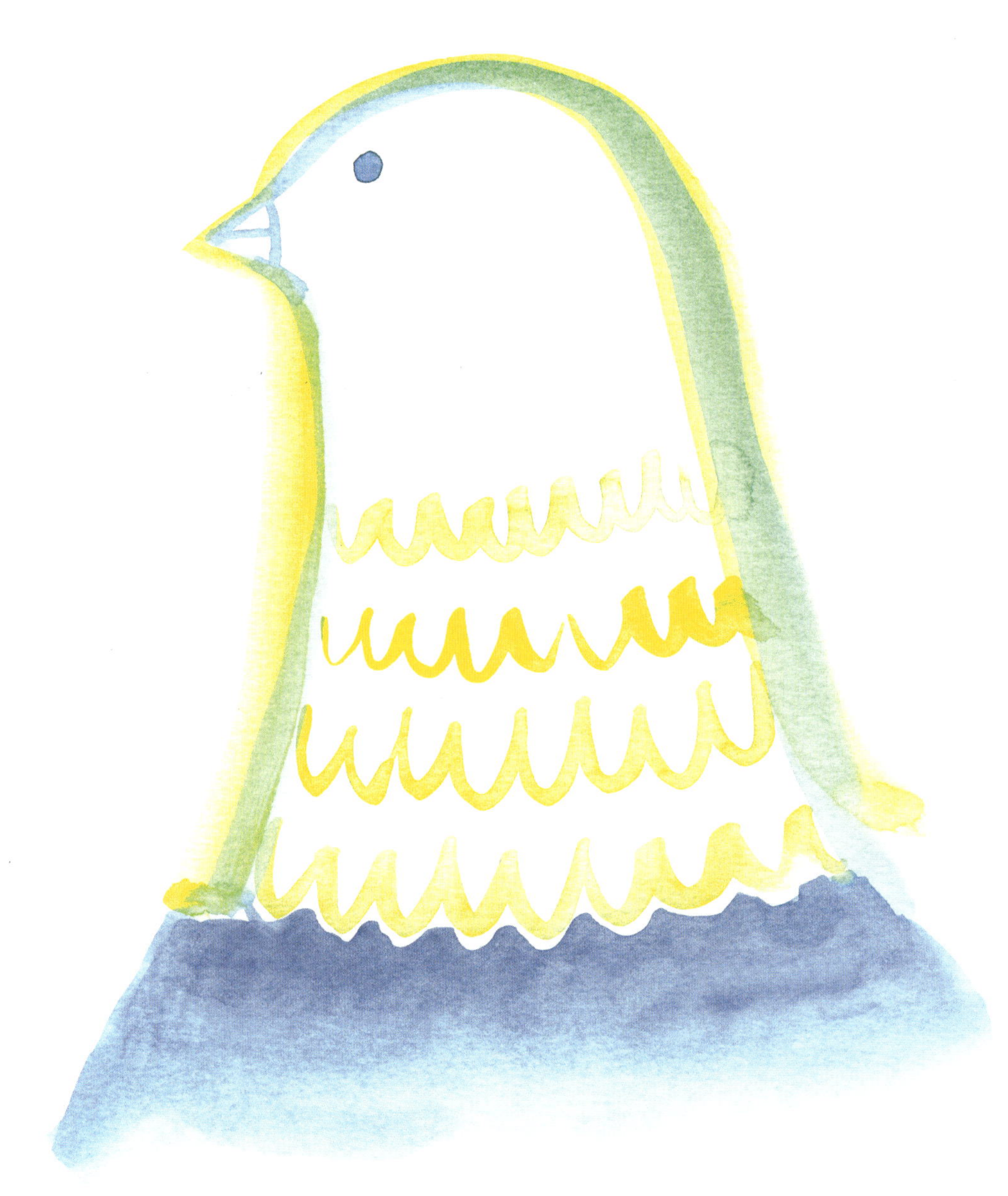

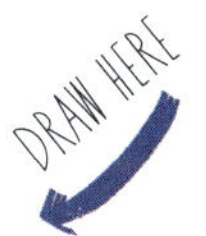

Choose an animal, either real or imaginary—or why not try a hybrid? Start sketching it above with your pens or brushes. It can be more of a character, a concept, an abstraction, or your shamanistic power animal! Have fun and don't judge the results. Use your pens to add details and play freely with your inks if you want to include bold splashes of color.

TIP: CHOOSE A CLOSE FRAME FOR IT IF YOU WANT TO GIVE YOUR ARTWORK A PORTRAIT VIBE OR DEPICT SEVERAL ISOLATED DETAILS OF ITS BODY IF YOU WANT TO GIVE IT A VINTAGE BIOLOGY CHART APPROACH.

COMPOSE AN IMAGE

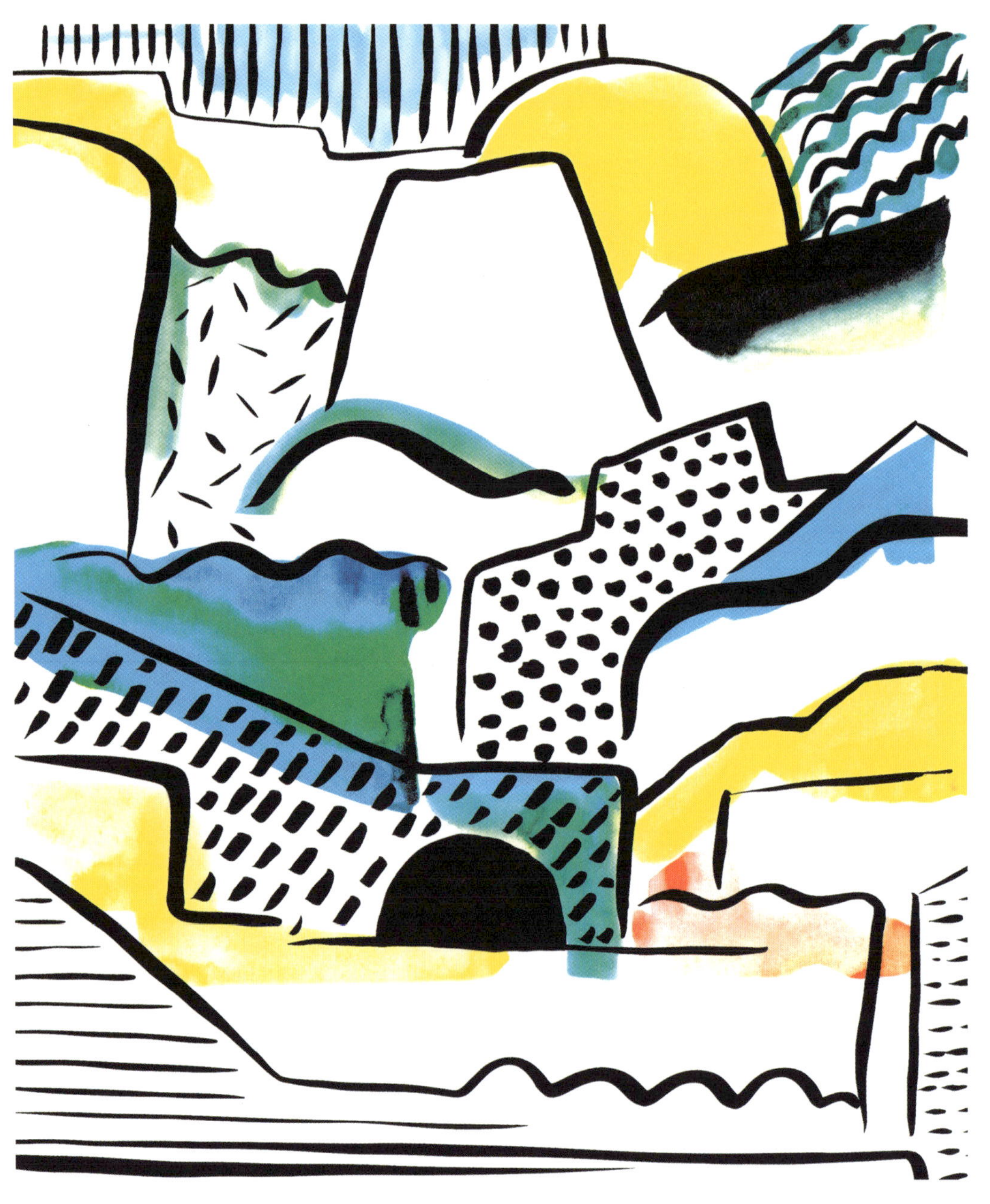

SKETCH AND PAINT HERE

A viewfinder can help you isolate and select the area of something, usually a landscape, you want to picture and sketch. It's more accurate if it has some gridlike marks. You can buy a viewfinder or make one yourself—see instructions below. Looking through it will help you frame the motif of your next painting or sketch. Let the image hunt begin!

TIP: TO MAKE A VIEWFINDER, CUT A HOLE IN THE MIDDLE OF A PIECE OF PAPER AND MAKE SOME MARKS AROUND THE BORDER OF THE PERFORATION TO DEFINE THE EDGES OF AN IMAGINARY GRID CROSSING THE HOLE.

REPEAT STENCIL

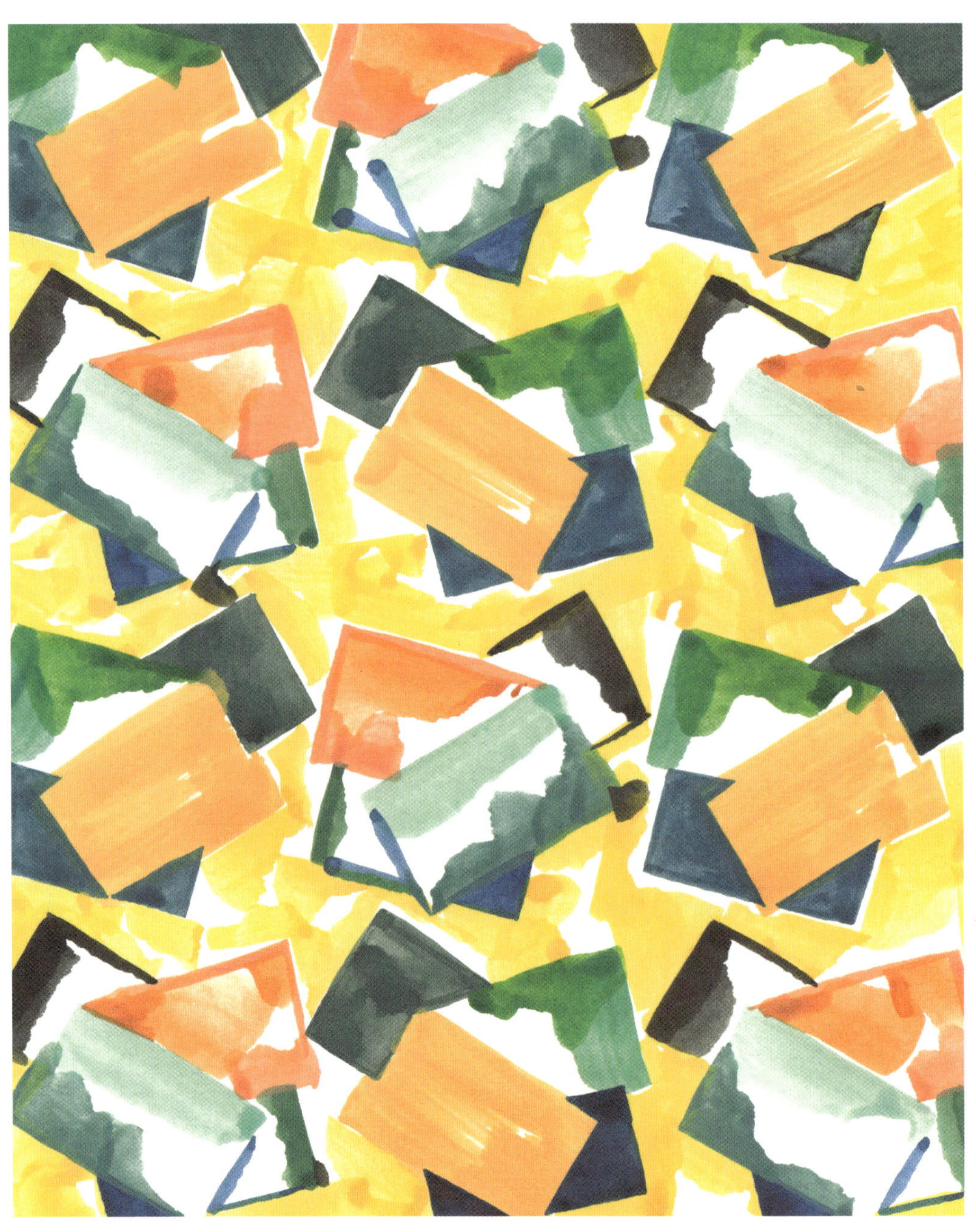

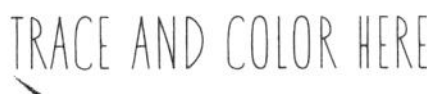

Create a simple drawing with your pencil on a thick paper or cardboard. With a craft knife, cut most of the outlines in the motif without separating it into different pieces. Make cuts parallel to the ones you just made in order to create lanes wide enough for your pencil tip. Take this stencil and trace those lines with a pencil in different positions above. Now experiment with color on the different areas you just outlined with your pencil!

TIP: WHEN POSITIONING YOUR STENCIL, TRY FLIPPING IT HORIZONTALLY AND VERTICALLY AND ROTATING IT AS MUCH AS YOU WANT. PLAY WITH THE COMPOSITION AND REPEAT RHYTHM TO CREATE YOUR UNIQUE PATTERN!

LINE DRAWING

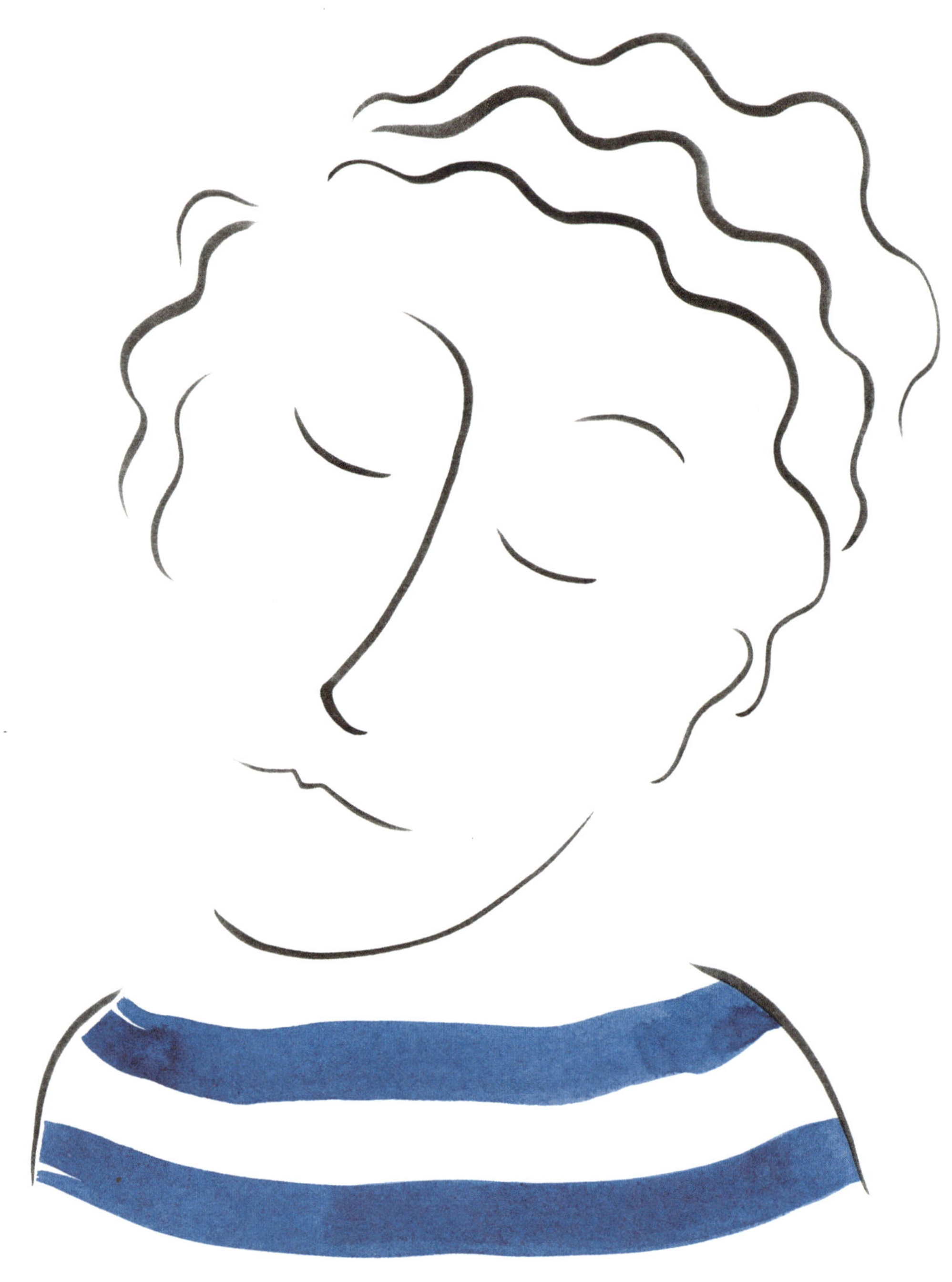

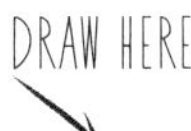

Try to express something or represent someone with as few marks as possible. Look at your model closely, choose the key features you want to paint, and start outlining them with a pencil. Focus just on the essentials. Feel free to make a few rough sketches until you are happy with the key marks. Try different sketches of the same subject, each with one less stroke and see whether you can make it to just two or three strokes.

TIP: ADD SOME BOLD DETAILS OR CONTRASTING COLORS TO BALANCE THE MINIMAL VIBE OF THE LINE DRAWING. CHECK SOME PICASSO DRAWINGS FOR LINE INSPIRATION; HE WAS AMAZING AT THAT.

WARM TO COLD

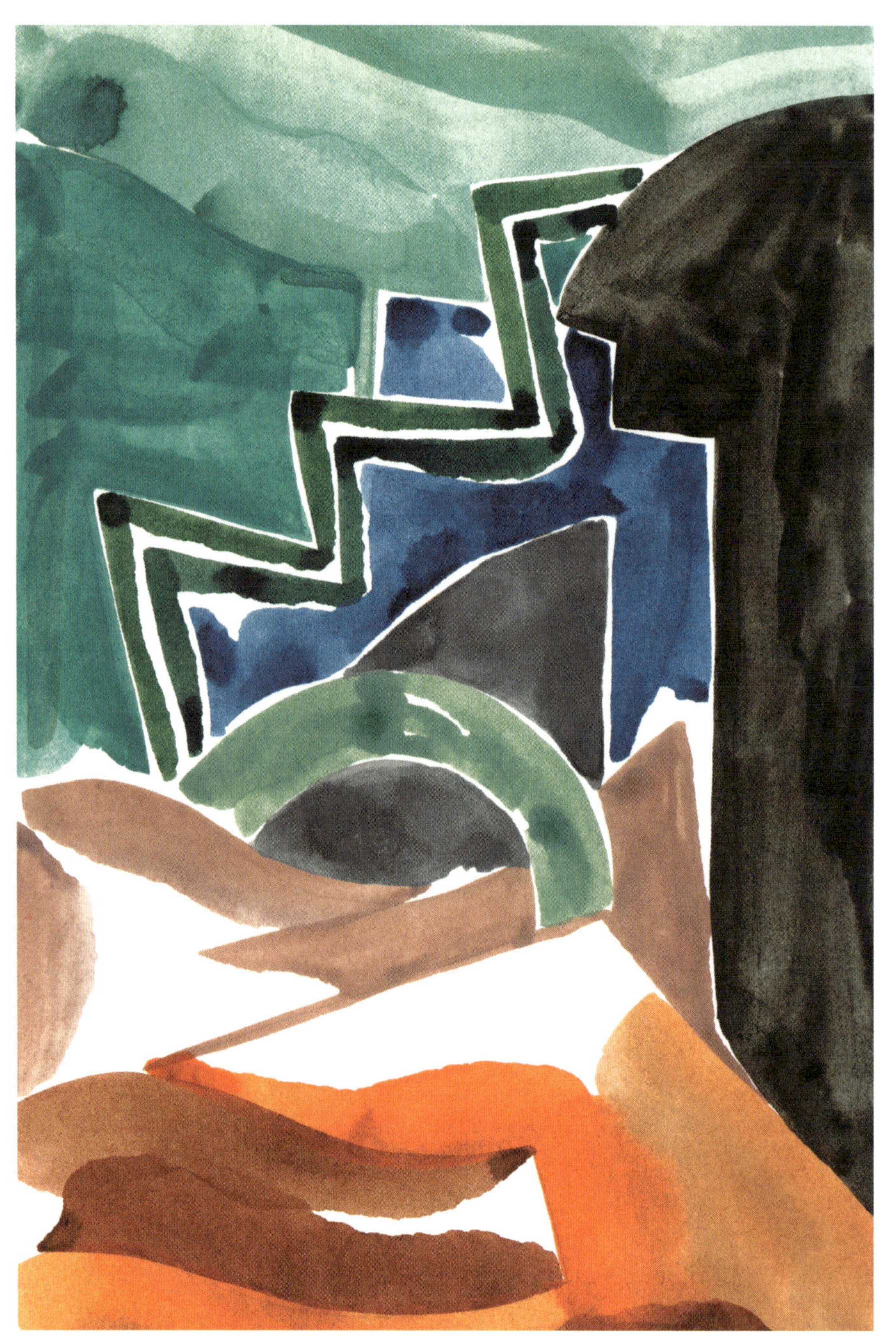

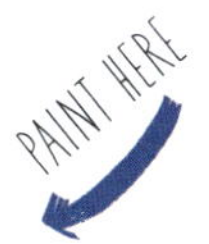

Color is a great tool to represent depth. Warmer colors tend to look as if they are closer to us than colder hues. Following this fact, try making a painting in which you explore depth just with your color palette. Your composition can be as abstract or as representational as you want. The key thing is to focus on the use of color.

TIP: FOR MORE SOPHISTICATED AND PERSONAL HUES, USE A PALETTE TO MIX DIFFERENT INKS. MAKE PASTELS BY ADDING WHITE, MUTE HUES BY ADDING A TOUCH OF BLACK OR THEIR COMPLEMENTARY COLORS, AND SO ON.

TINY ELEMENTS

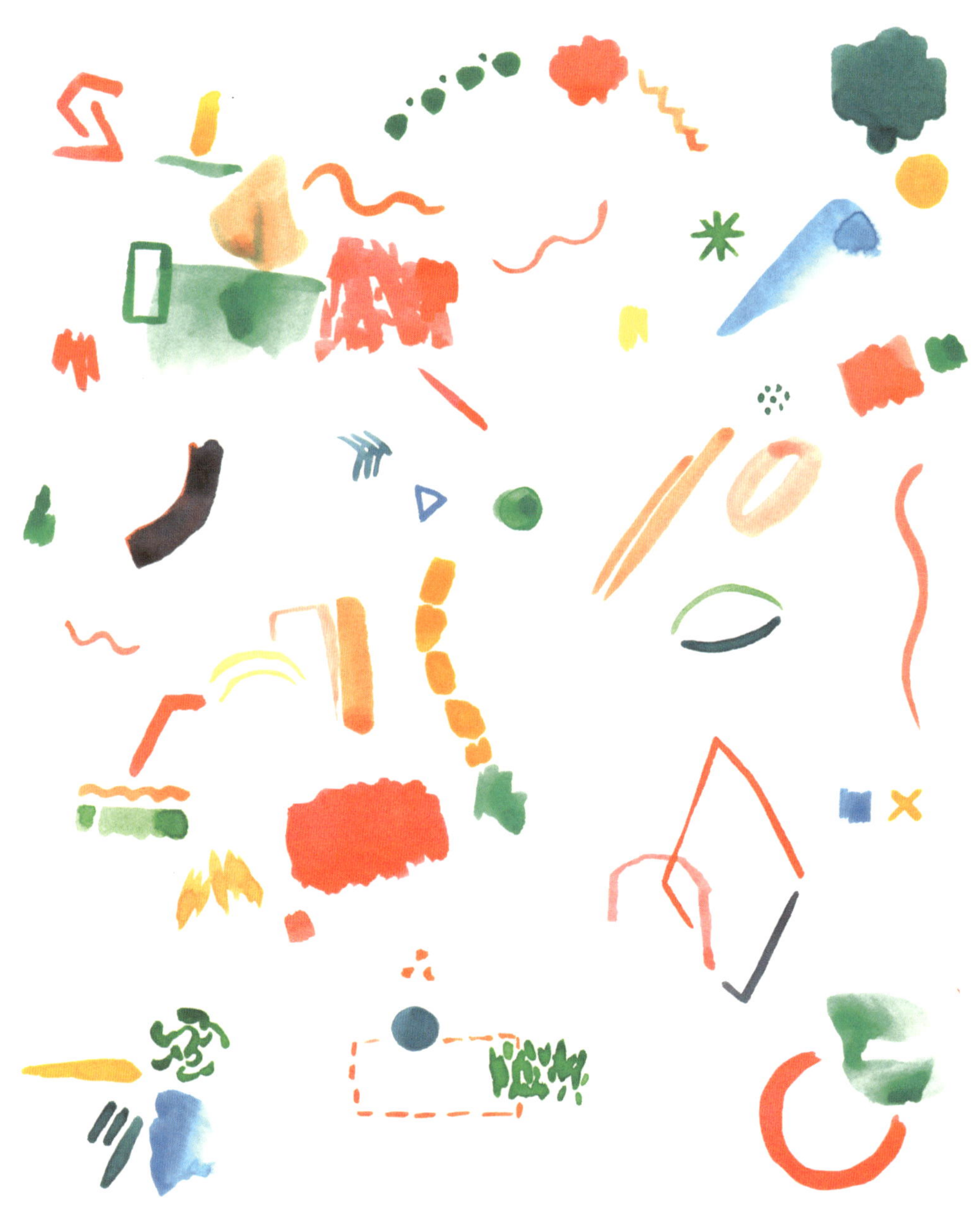

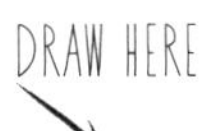

Create a pattern using a wide range of tiny elements. They can be abstract or you can go all representational and paint tiny people, houses, cars, or anything else in different positions and hues. Notice the rhythm of the repetition in your composition while filling your page. If you want your painting to have a colored background, color it first!

TIP: FOR INSPIRATION, SEARCH "UNDER THE MICROSCOPE" ONLINE FOR A PEEK INTO THE MICRO WORLD AND ITS SHAPES. SAND UNDER THE MICROSCOPE IS BEYOND BEAUTIFUL, FOR EXAMPLE.

LINE AND WASH

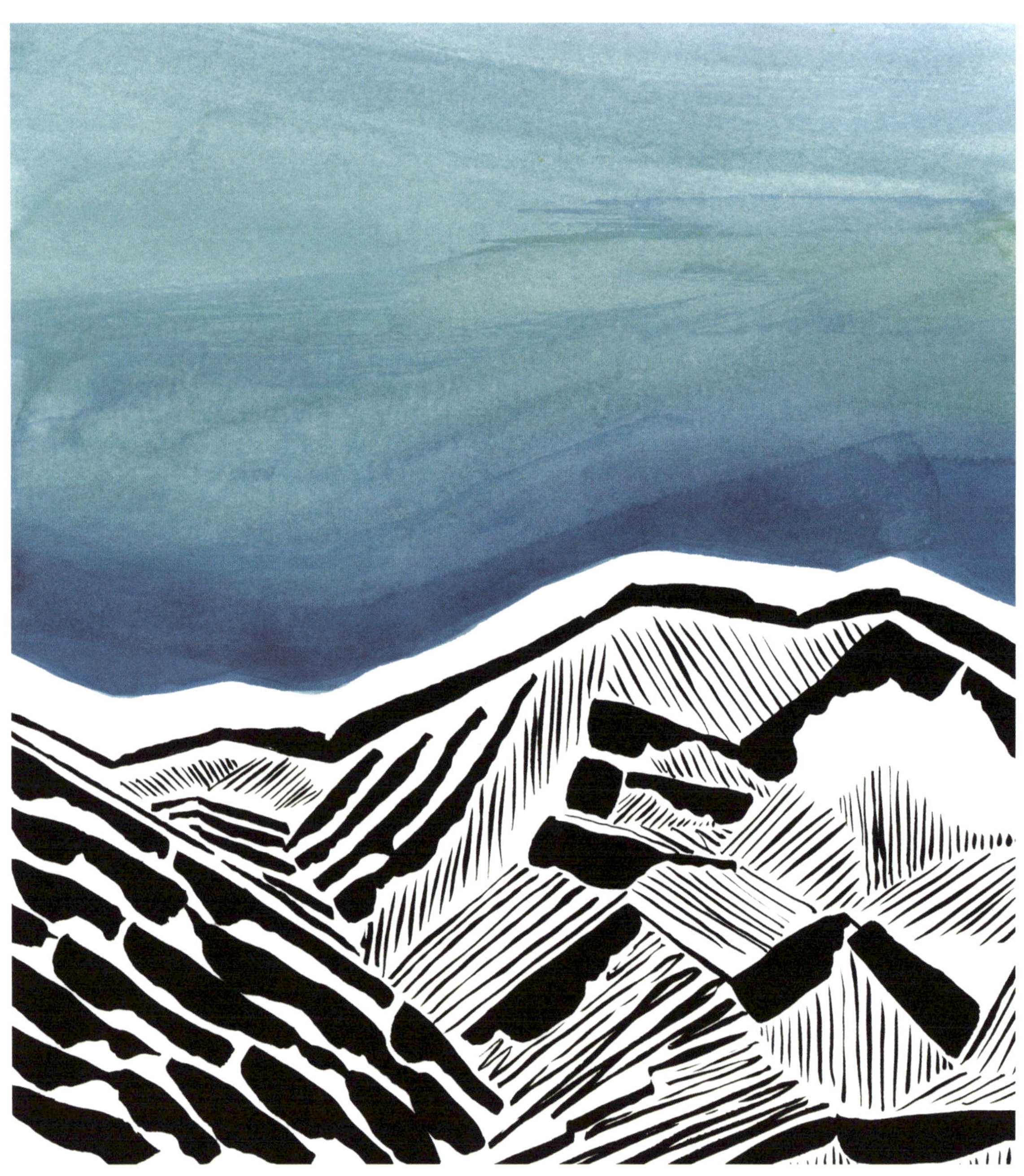

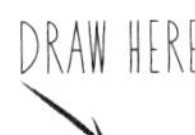

Let's play with two different languages. Outline a motif/landscape/figure you like above and choose which areas you'll add lines and strokes to and which will be filled just with color washes. Be quick when applying the washes if you want them to blend and have fun playing with the different line qualities on the textured areas.

TIP: TO MAKE LINES WITH DIFFERENT THICKNESSES, PLAY WITH THE ANGLE OF YOUR BRUSH. THE MORE PERPENDICULAR YOUR BRUSH IS TO THE PAPER, THE THINNER THE LINES WILL BE—AND VICE VERSA.

SPIRAL VIEW

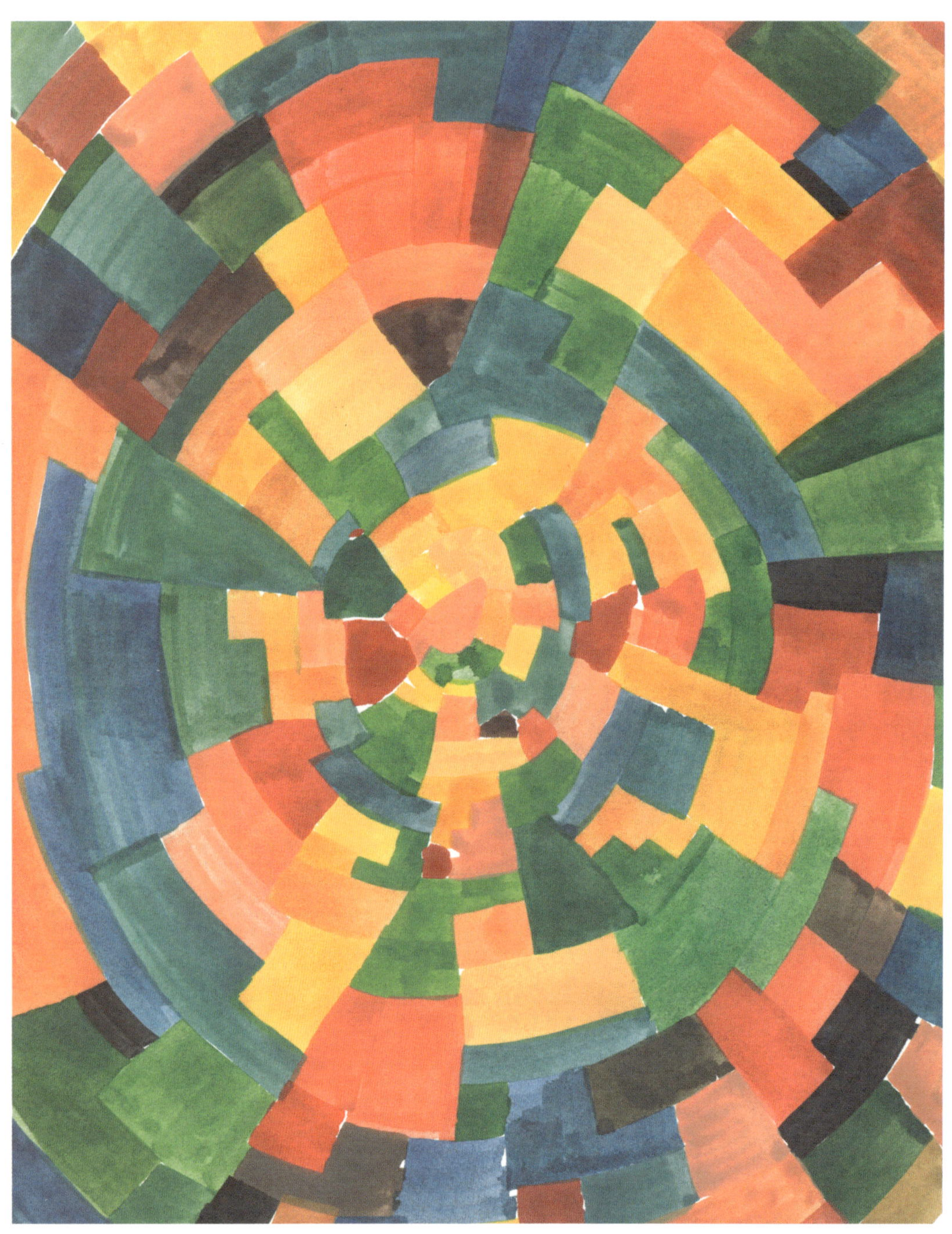

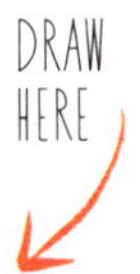

Many things follow a spiral construction, from flowers to crystals to endless man-made objects. Choose or invent one for this exercise. My artwork, for example, was inspired by one of those Earth aerial views featuring patches of land side by side arranged in a helical structure. Use a flat brush if you want to keep your strokes rectangular.

TIP: YOU CAN PAINT DIRECTLY WITH INK INSTEAD OF PLANNING AND OUTLINING YOUR COMPOSITION. JUST START IN THE CENTER AND ORGANICALLY GROW YOUR PAINTING FROM IT. IT WILL BE EASY AND GIVE IT A WHIRLWIND MOTION.

LINE BOTANICALS

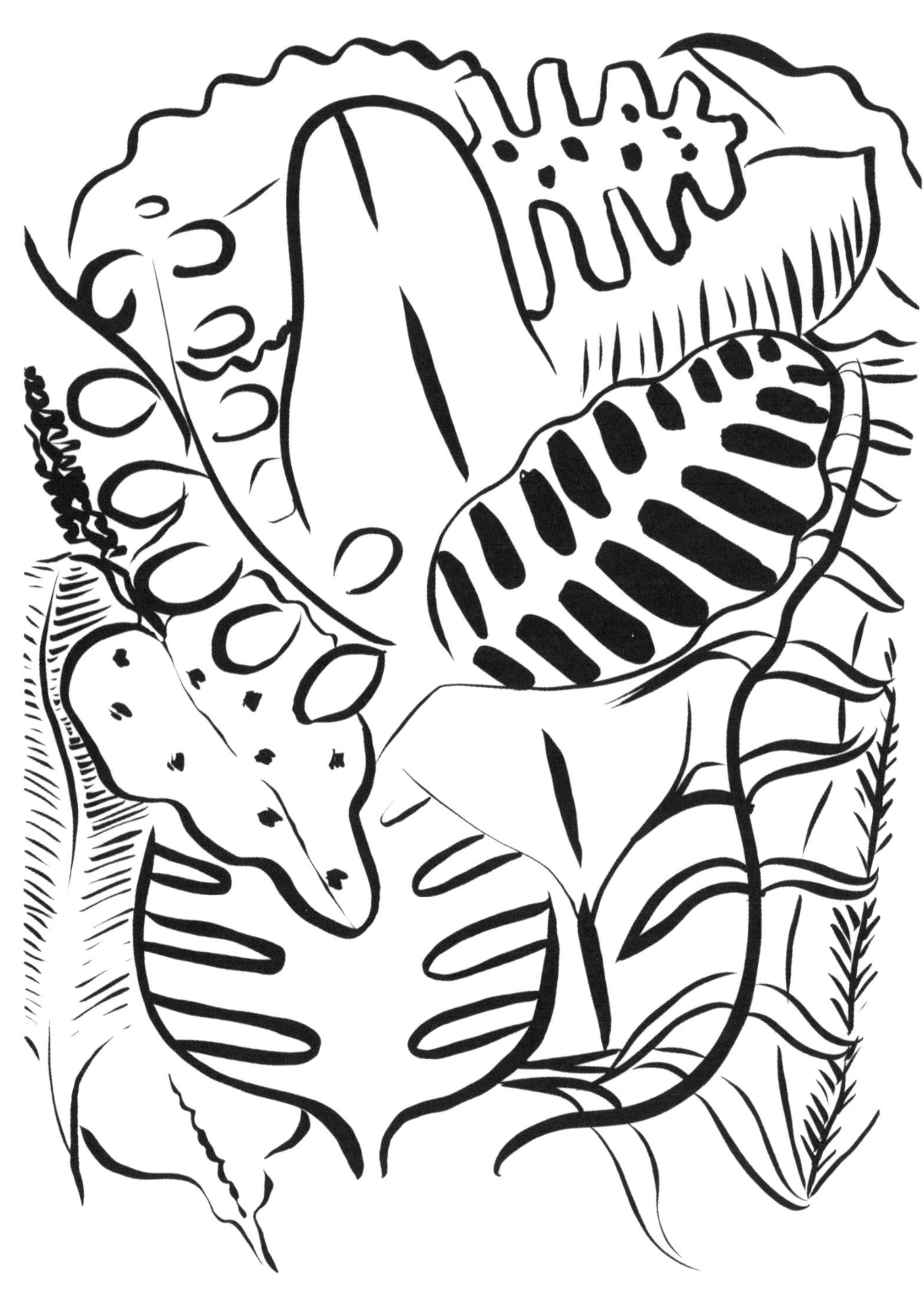

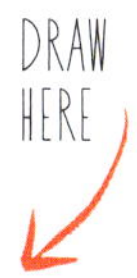

Go for a walk in a garden or park that you like. Notice the greenery around you. Choose your favorite specimens and start sketching an arrangement made out of them above. Draw their outlines using a pencil. Use a brush and ink to outline them or apply color. Start with simple lines but go as detailed as you want. The key here is to get familiar with the shapes of the plants and see how they behave when placed together.

TIP: IF NO PARK OR INSPIRING GARDEN IS AVAILABLE TO YOU, TREAT YOURSELF AND BUY A FLOWER BOUQUET THAT CATCHES YOUR EYE TO USE AS A MODEL INSTEAD.

PLASTIC WRAP

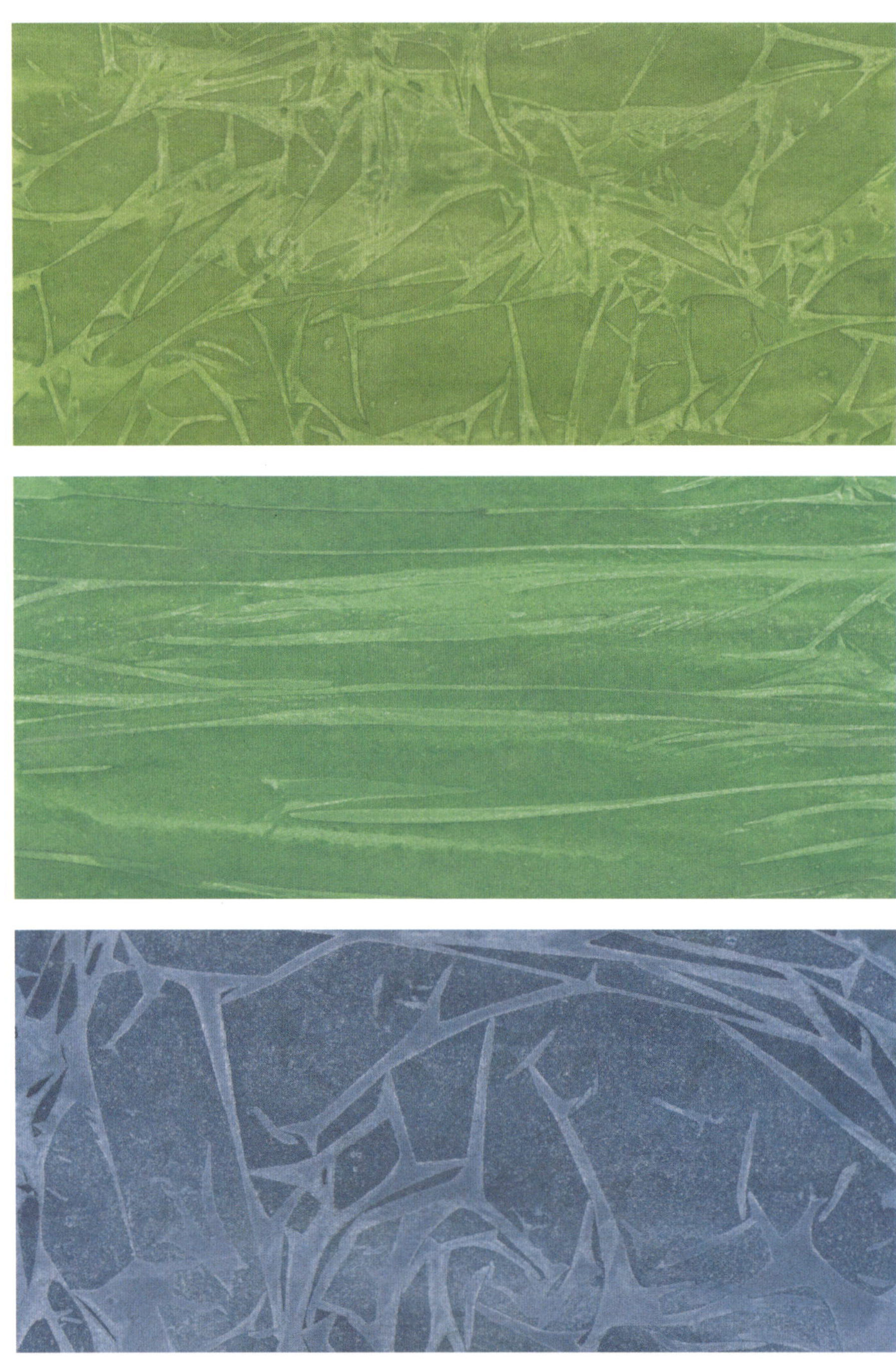

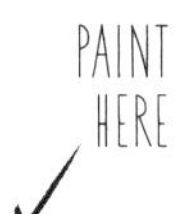

Plastic wrap can give an interesting texture to a color wash or painting and it's easy to work with. Just lay a piece of plastic wrap on top of the ink while it's still wet. Play with its wrinkles and leave it alone once you find a texture you like. Wait for the ink to dry, remove the plastic wrap, and view your results!

TIP: THE PLASTIC WRAP CAN BE STRETCHED, CREASED, PERFORATED, ROTATED, WRINKLED, AND SO ON TO ACHIEVE THE TEXTURES AND FORMS YOU WANT TO CREATE FOR YOUR PAINTING. EXPERIMENT AND HAVE FUN!

A PICTURE WITHIN A PICTURE

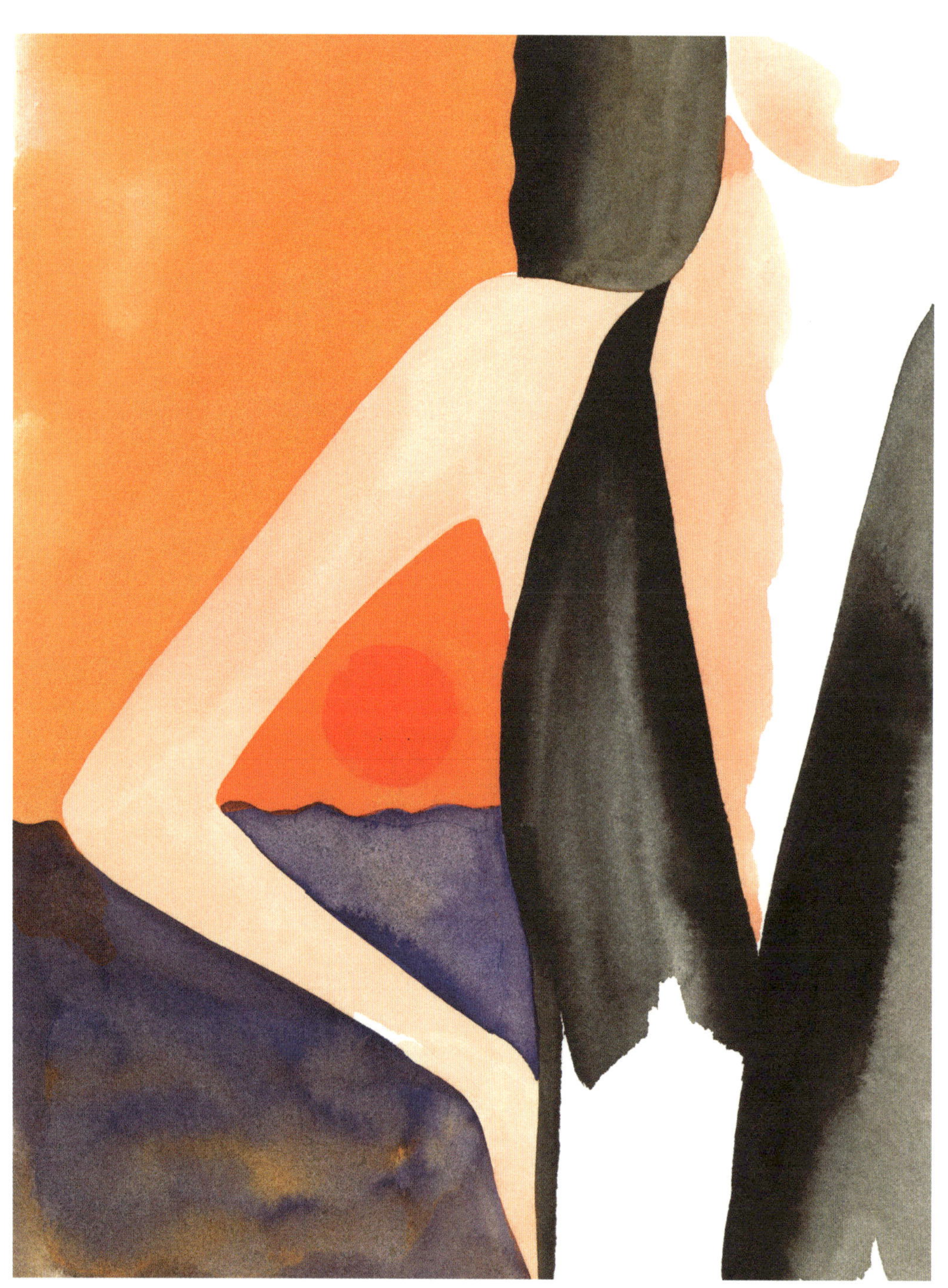

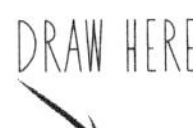

Our environment contains many frames—empty spaces between buildings, gaps between greenery or rocks, and so on. This exercise is like an organic alternative to the viewfinder one on page 43. Plan a painting with a very defined foreground and background. It can be close-up leaves on a bush with a village in the background, for example, or a piece of landscape seen through the gap of your friend's arm. Don't put pressure on yourself and try to keep it simple. The key here is to experiment framing within the frame!

TIP: THINK OF THE BACKGROUND AS A PAINTING WITHIN A PAINTING. USE DIFFERENT TECHNIQUES AND COLOR TONES TO HELP IT STAND OUT MORE FROM THE FOREGROUND.

TEXTURING WITH FABRIC

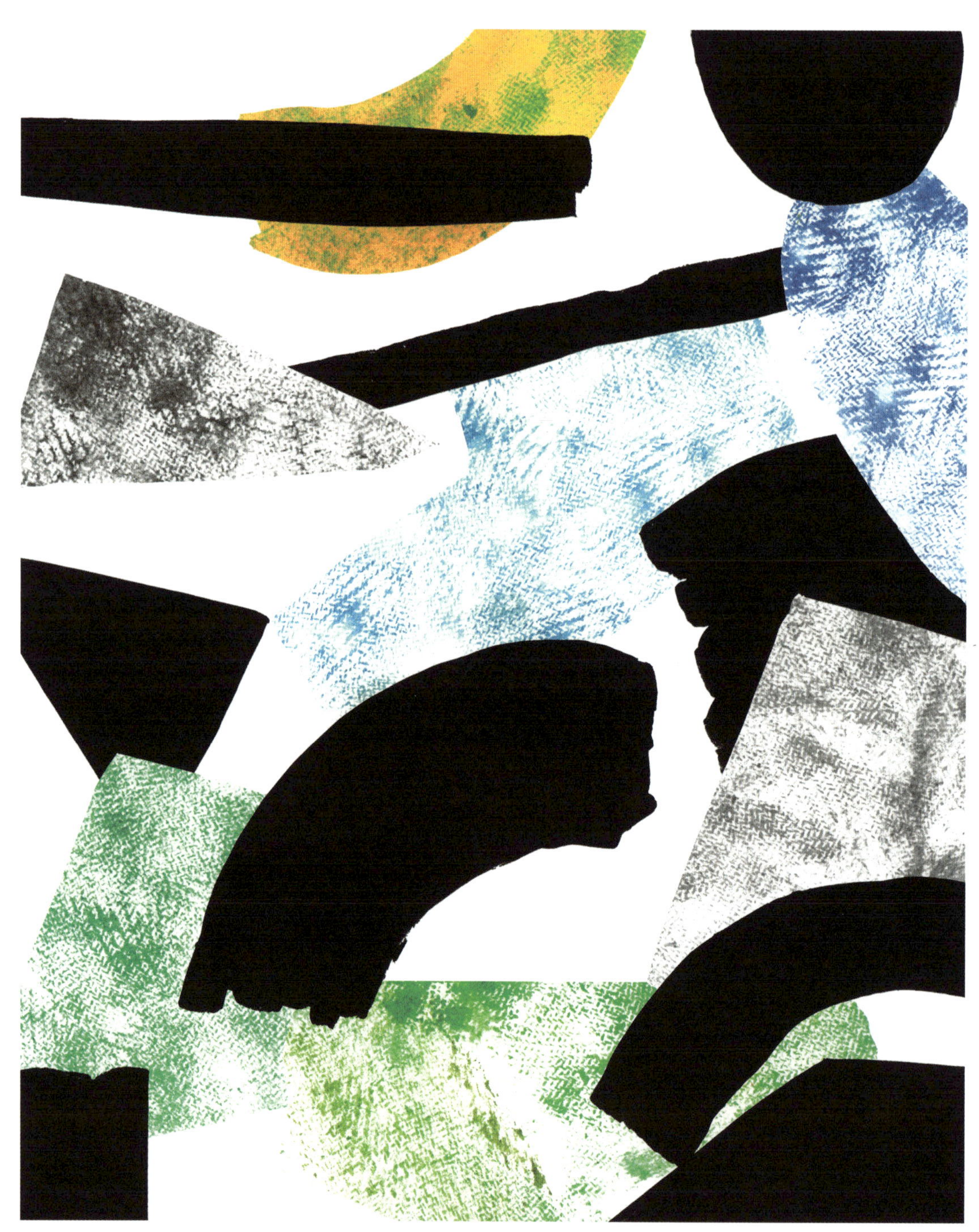

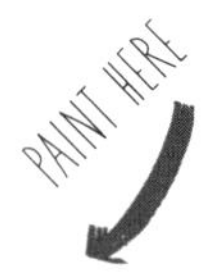

Fabric can create very interesting textures in your artwork. Start a painting. While the ink is still wet, press a piece of fabric on top of one of the areas to remove a bit of the color and create a lighter texture. If you are using watercolor paper, the texture may be very subtle so try the experiment in the opposite way: Press the piece of fabric onto wet ink first so that you can use it as a stamp on dry areas of your painting.

TIP: TRY DIFFERENT KINDS OF FABRIC FOR THIS EXERCISE. EACH ONE OF THEM WILL GIVE YOU A UNIQUE TEXTURE. UPHOLSTERY FABRICS, FOR EXAMPLE, CAN GIVE YOU VERY DEFINED, CRISP PATTERNS.

ESCHER TESSELLATION

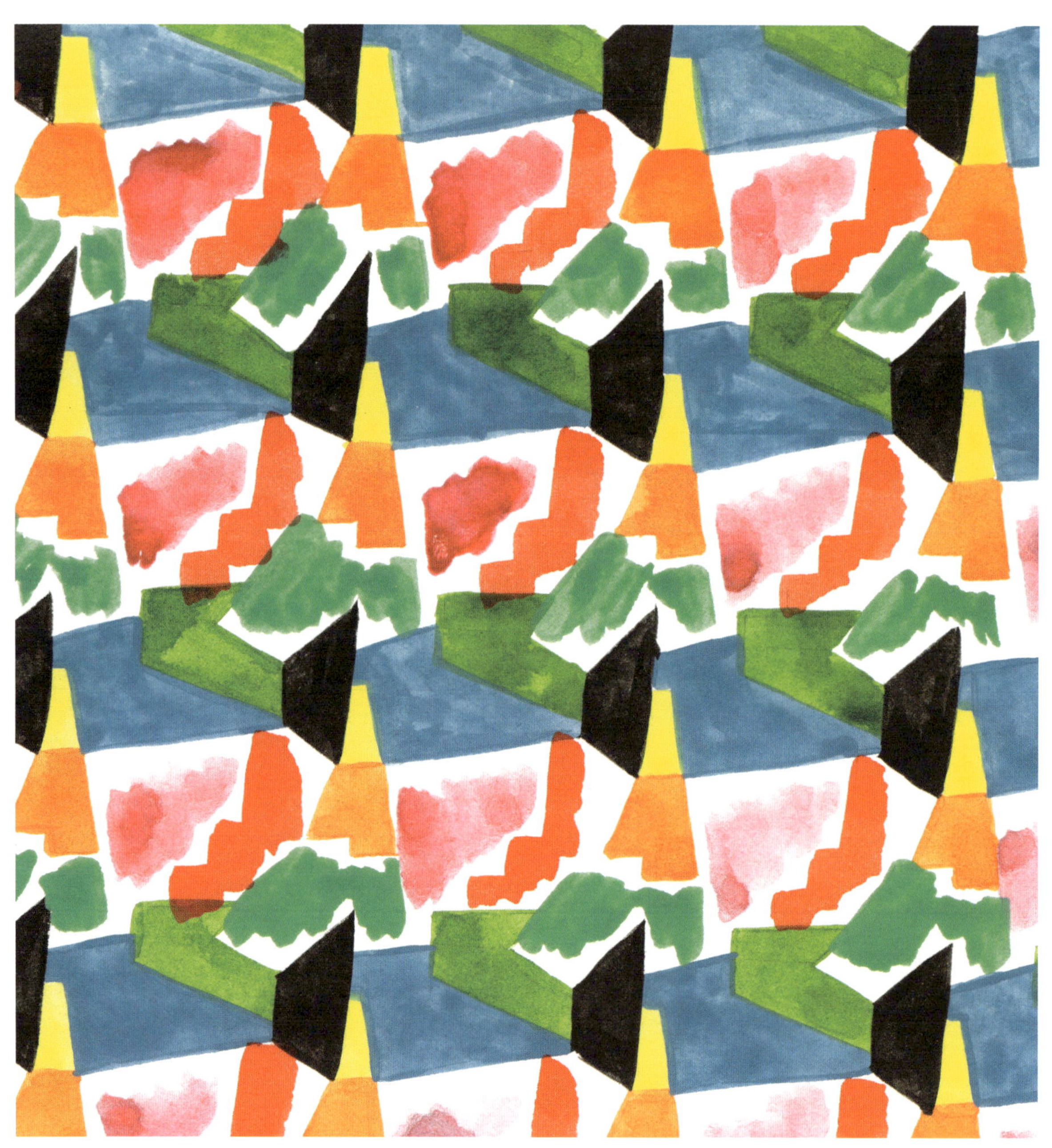

TRACE AND COLOR HERE

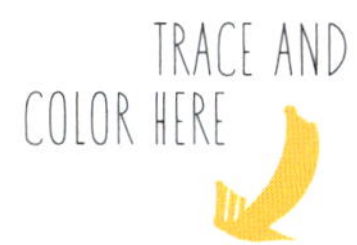

Cut a square piece out of cardstock or thick paper. Cut a shape at the top with a pair of scissors or a craft knife. Do the same on one of the sides. Tape the top piece on the bottom of the square and the other piece to the opposite side. Trace the contour of the cardstock piece with your pencil on a piece of paper or above. Repeat the process, tracing the contours side by side to form a puzzlelike pattern with all the pieces fitting exactly. Now you are ready to color with your pen and inks!

TIP: THE SAMPLE ARTWORK ON THE OPPOSITE PAGE IS PRETTY ABSTRACT BUT BELIEVE ME, EVEN THE MOST ABSTRACT SHAPES CAN BECOME ANIMALS, FACES, OR OTHER MOTIFS FOR YOUR PATTERN TO BE REPRESENTATIONAL. GIVE IT A TRY!

MASKING TAPE STRIPES

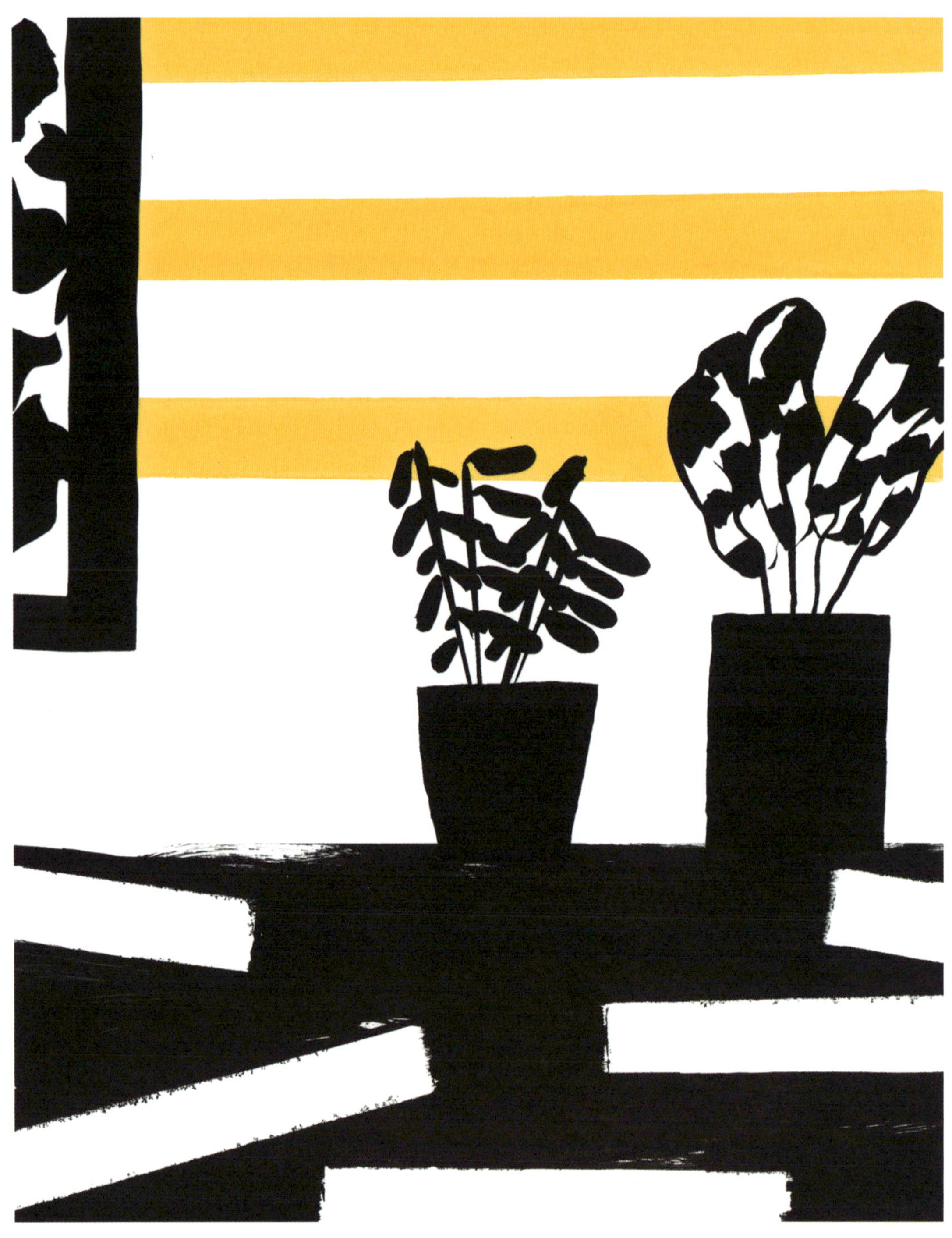

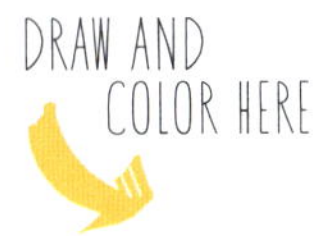

Outline a drawing with your pencil and choose a few areas that you'd like to keep free of ink. Apply masking tape to those areas and start coloring on the tape-free areas. Apply pressure to the edges of the masking tape to secure them so that the ink doesn't leak underneath. When the ink is dry, remove the tape gently so you don't damage the paper and add more details to your painting with your brushes and/or pens.

TIP: YOU CAN ALSO EXPERIMENT BY CUTTING THE MASKING TAPE WITH A CRAFT KNIFE TO ACHIEVE DIFFERENT SHAPES. FOR IRREGULAR SHAPES, YOU CAN SLIGHTLY OVERLAP SEVERAL PIECES OF TAPE BEFORE COLORING.

A TWO-COLOR SCARF

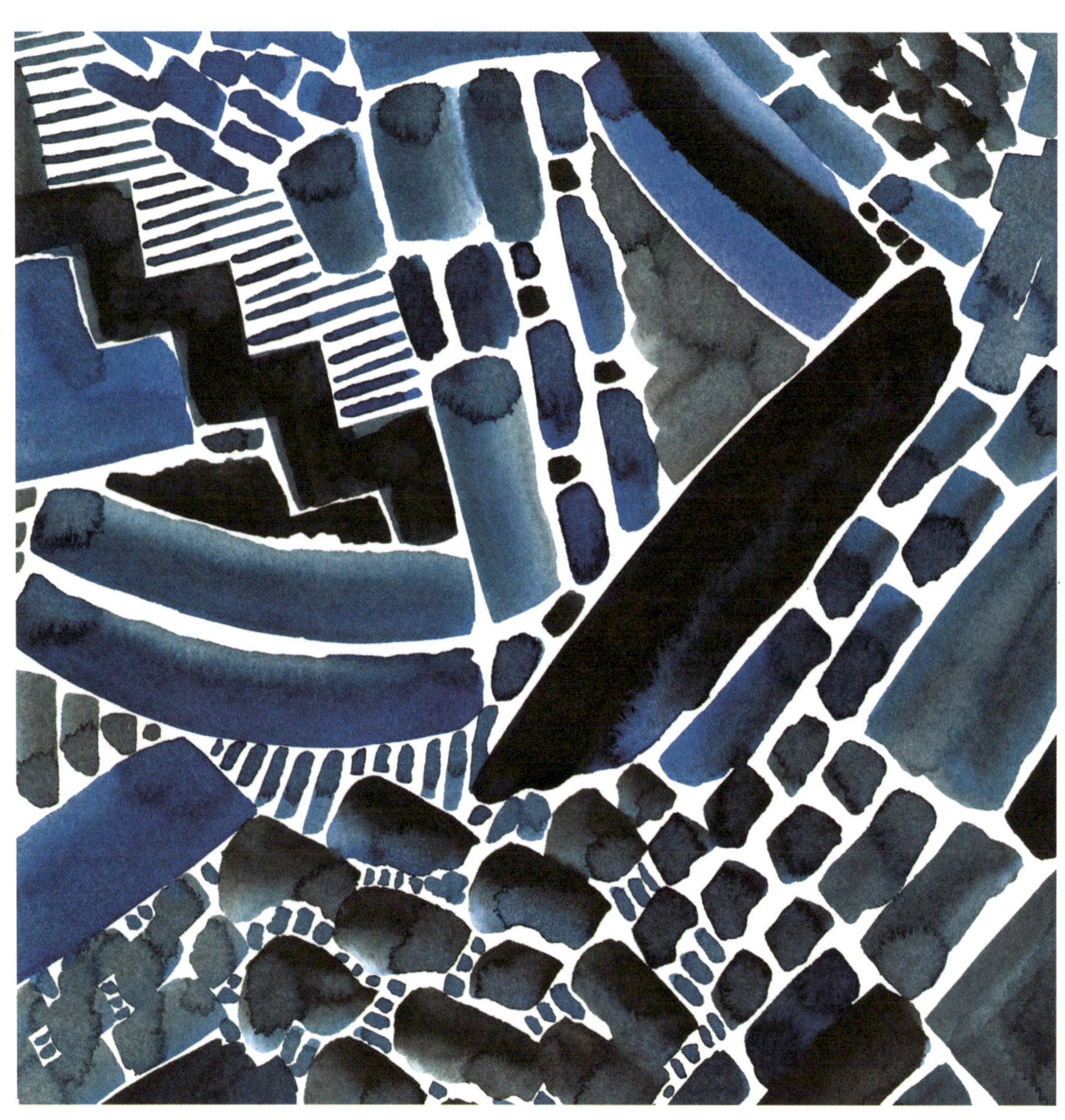

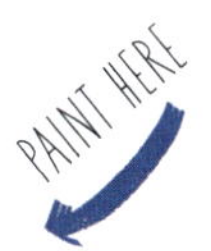

Color restriction can be a blessing in disguise. Having to think less about color helps you focus on form and composition. Create a painting or pattern above with just two colors to decorate a scarf you'd love to wear. Try different brushes or pens to play with different widths and finishes. It's totally fine to mix the colors you chose to have extra shades!

TIP: YOUR SCARF CAN BE A RECTANGLE, SQUARE, LONG BAND, OR SOMETHING SIMILAR. CHOOSE THE FORMAT THAT YOU THINK WILL WORK BEST WITH THE DESIGN YOU HAVE IN MIND.

INK COLLAGE

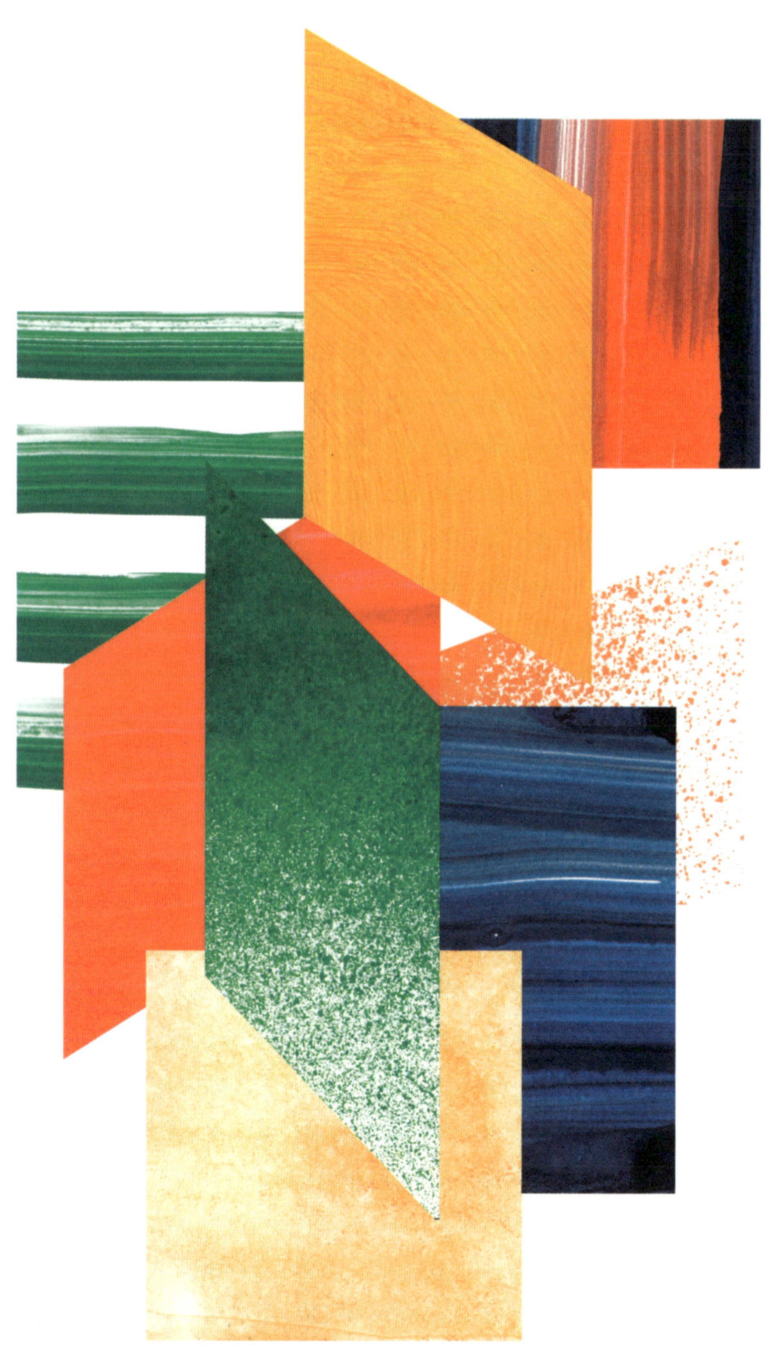

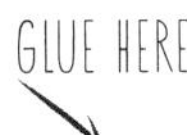

Find pieces of used paper, such as paintings and sketches that didn't turn out as you expected. Place them together and glue them onto a sheet of paper or above. If you want to give an impression of depth in the composition, make angular cuts to some of the pieces and arrange them accordingly to create this perspective.

TIP: FOR COLLAGE WORK, ALWAYS TRY USING NONTOXIC GLUE. COCCOINA, FOR EXAMPLE, IS A GREAT ONE AND BECAUSE IT'S ALMOND-BASED, IT EVEN SMELLS GOOD!

DRAW A MAP

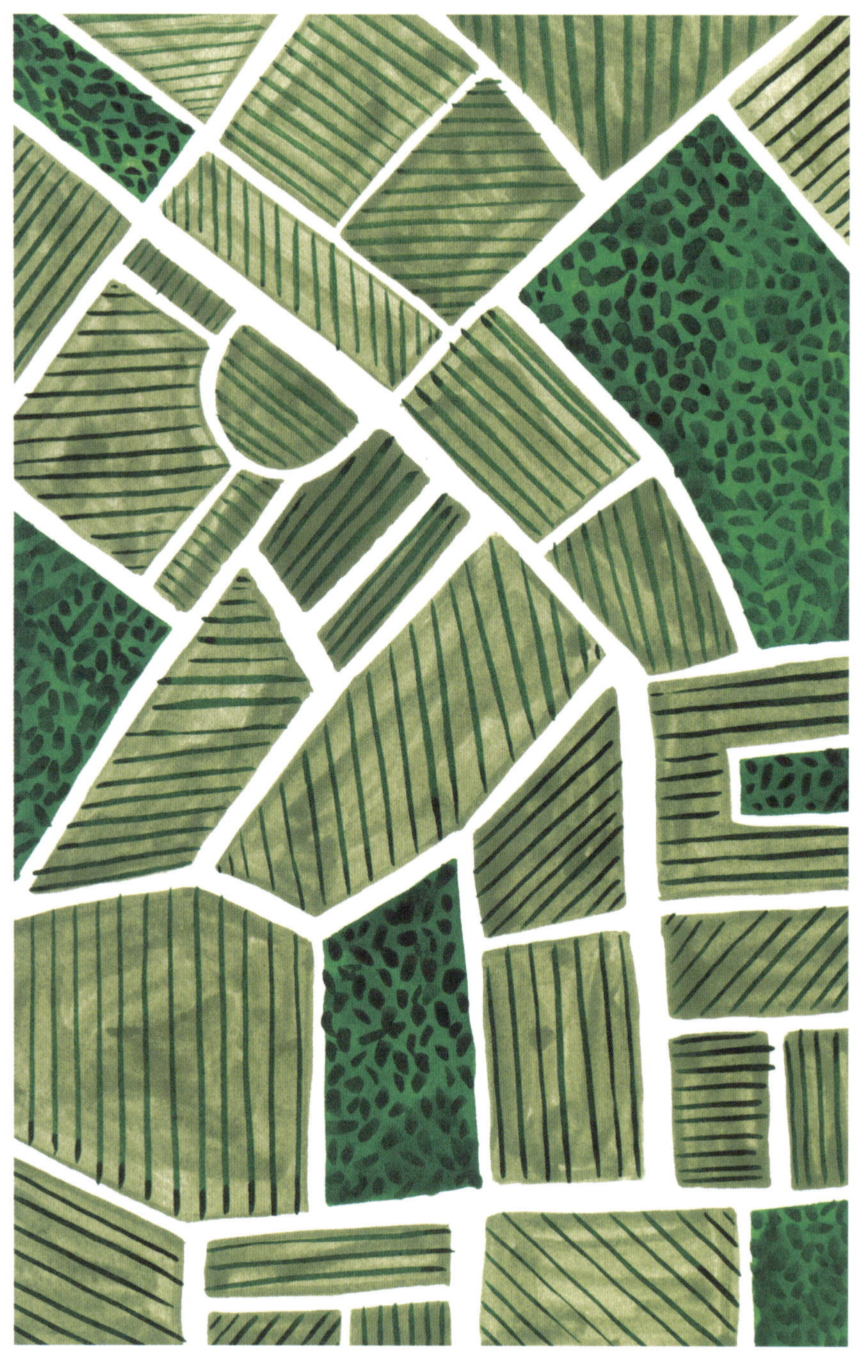

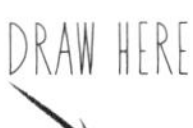

Let's make a map, but it doesn't have to be of a real place! For example, picture it as a treasure map to help you go from one place to the other. The places can be real or more abstract, such as states of being or goals. If you are into mazes, then go for a classic city map, always full of paths and patternlike repetitions of blocks.

TIP: TRY MAKING UP NONEXISTENT PLACES FOR YOUR MAP AS IF YOU WERE ABOUT TO EMBARK ON A HOBBITLIKE QUEST. ALSO FEEL FREE TO USE PERSPECTIVE, WORDS, OR SYMBOLS TO ADD MORE INFORMATION TO IT.

PAINTING WITH A SCRAPER

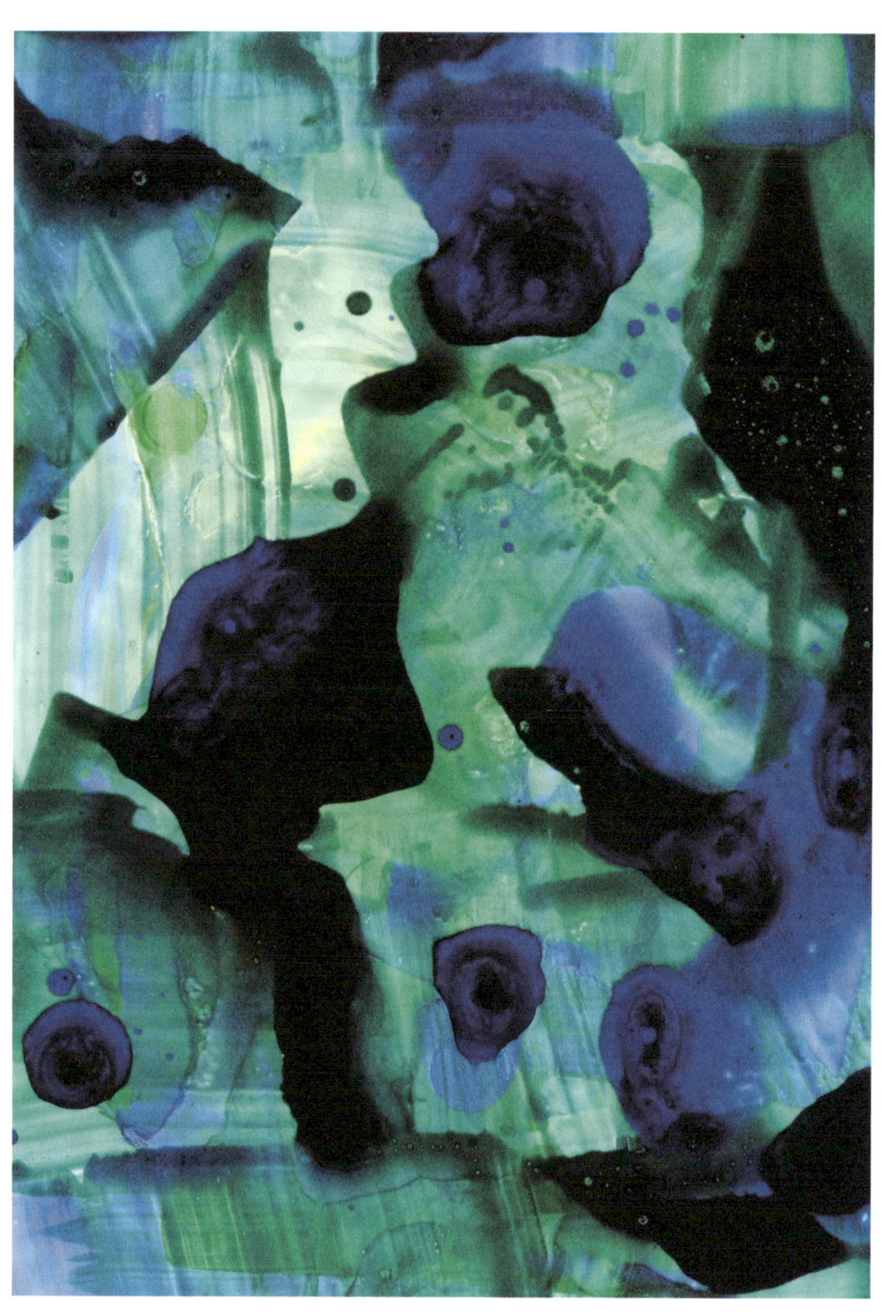

If you are doing this exercise with alcohol-based inks as I did, be sure to use synthetic paper such as Yupo or heavyweight coated paper. With the help of a dropper, apply different inks to the surface of the paper. Before the ink dries, take an old credit card or rigid piece of plastic and scrape the color with it to give your artwork shape and to mix the hues. When the ink is dry, repeat the process as many times as you want to layer on different shapes and colors.

TIP: FEEL FREE TO USE WATER-BASED INKS INSTEAD OF ALCOHOL-BASED ONES IF YOU PREFER. JUST BE SURE TO USE ABSORBENT PAPER AND WORK FAST SO THE INK ISN'T SOAKED UP IMMEDIATELY.

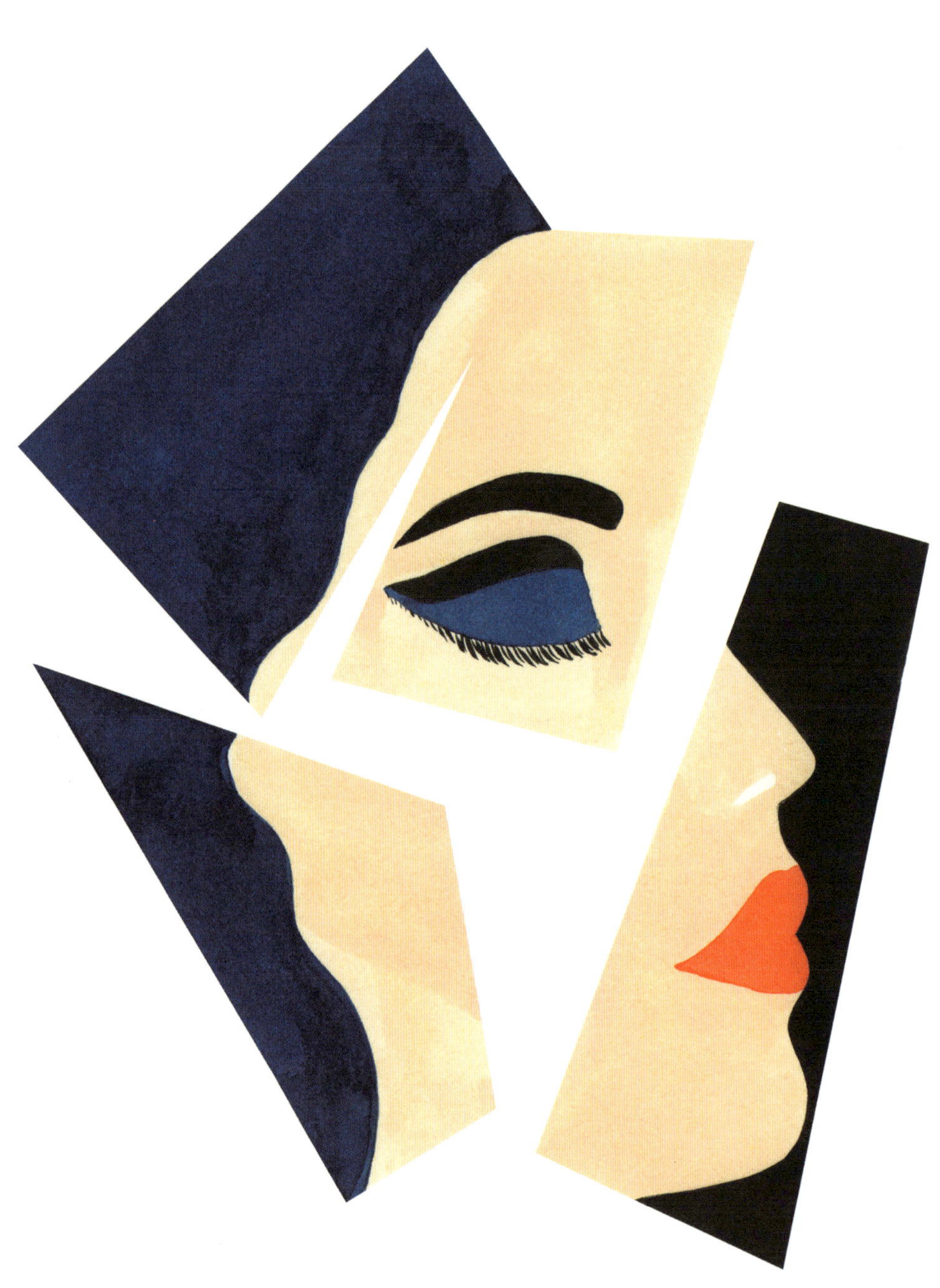

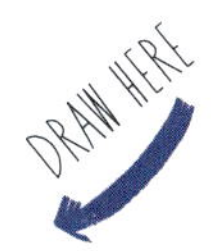

Sketch something that you like and draw frames around some areas of the image with your pencil. Erase the areas of the drawing that are not framed and start coloring the ones that are. Framing can make your artwork bolder and more iconic. Give it a try!

TIP: THE FRAMES CAN HAVE THE SHAPES YOU WANT. THEY CAN BE REGULAR OR IRREGULAR SHAPES, ABSTRACT OR REPRESENTATIONAL, SUCH AS THE CLASSIC KEYHOLE. YOU CHOOSE!

CORALS

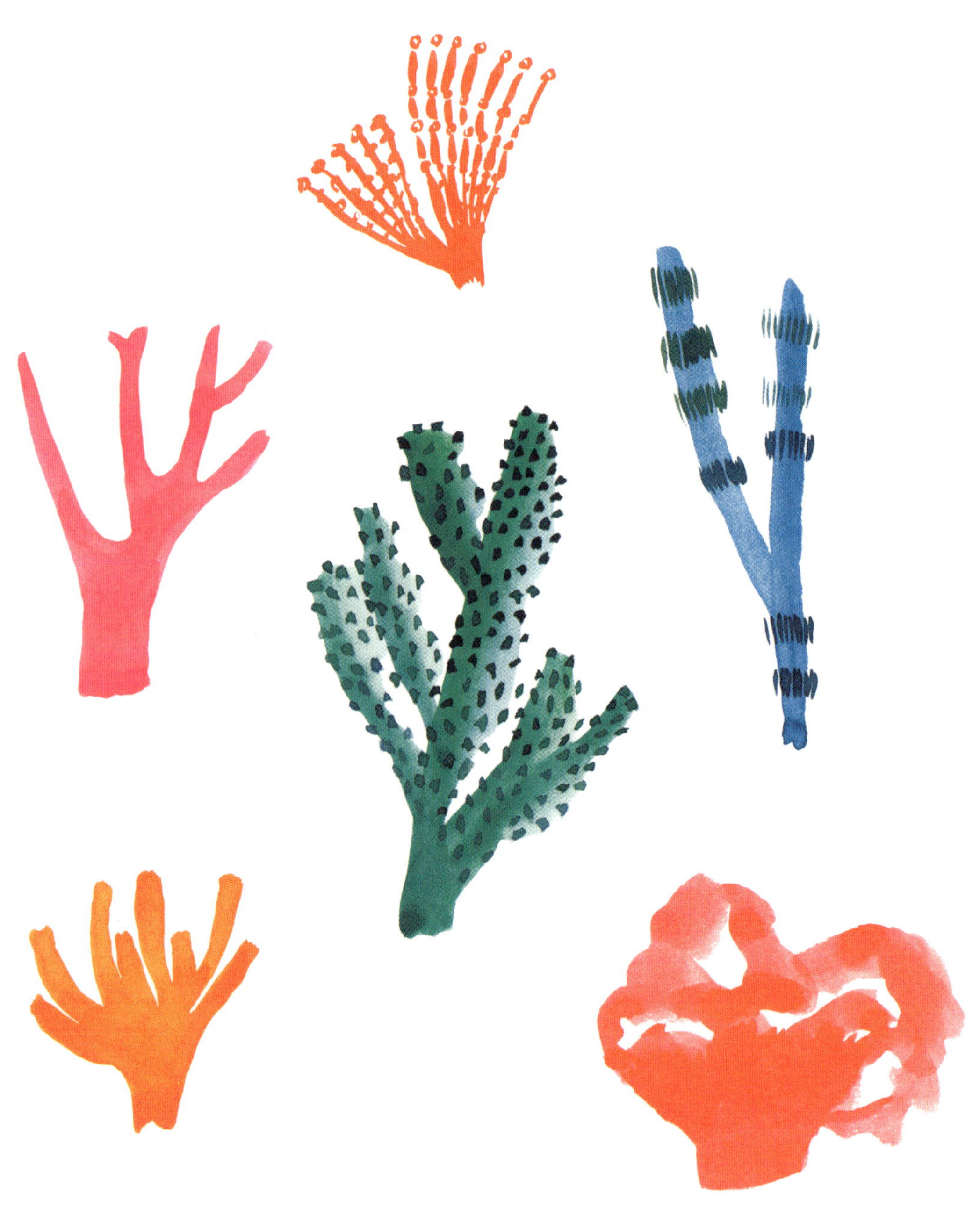

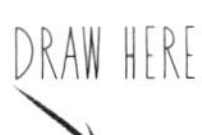

Look at pictures of coral reefs. Choose some examples that you like—or make up some of your own. Use different pens and brushes to achieve a wide range of finishes. Flat brushes can help with even strokes, thin ones work great to make tiny dot textures, fan brushes are ideal for palmlike shapes, and so on.

TIP: MAKE SOME BASIC SHAPES WITH YOUR BRUSH. WHEN DRY, ADD DETAILS ON TOP OF THEM WITH YOUR PEN TO GIVE PERSONALITY TO EACH OF THE CORALS. APPLY A LIGHT BLUE WASH ON TOP FOR AN UNDERWATER EFFECT.

LET'S GET TECHNICAL

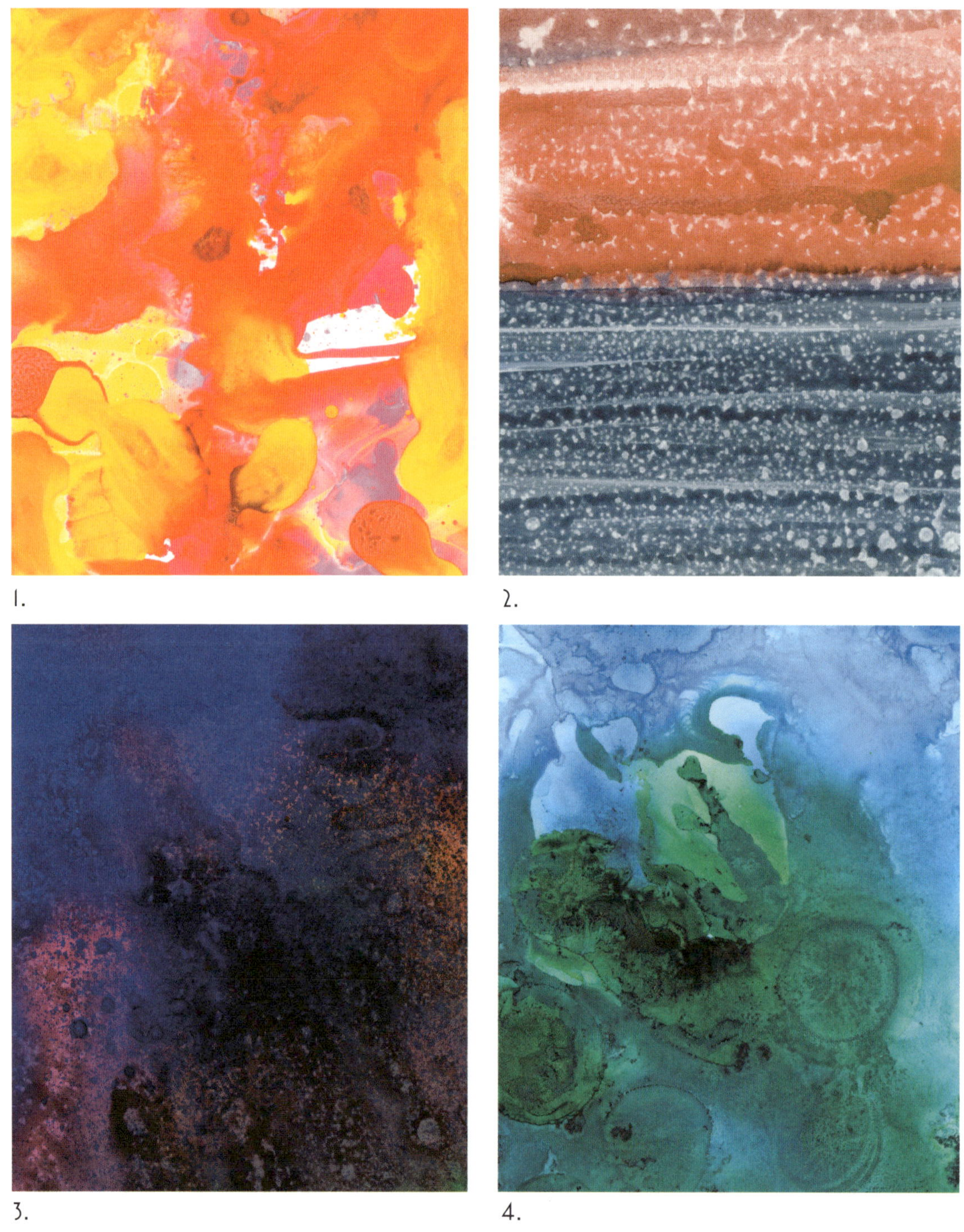

1.

2.

3.

4.

APPLY INK HERE

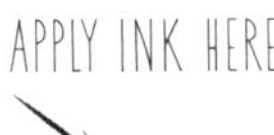

Here are some specific techniques to try with alcohol-based or water-based inks mixed with rubbing alcohol. 1. Alcohol-based ink applied with a scraper with extra ink drops on top to saturate the color. 2. Rubbing alcohol sprayed on top of wet washes of water-based ink. 3. Alcohol-based ink applied with a dropper on top of blending solution alcohol, and afterward sprayed with ultramarine alcohol-based ink. 4. Rubbing alcohol sprayed on synthetic paper such as Yupo, alcohol-based inks applied with droppers afterward, and extra rubbing alcohol sprayed on top of all to activate the mixture.

TIP: ALCOHOL-BASED INK CAN BE EASILY APPLIED AND SPREAD JUST BY ADDING A COUPLE OF DROPS TO A PIECE OF FELT THAT CAN BE USED AS A STAMP OR BRUSH. A LITTLE INK GOES A LONG WAY!

GRIDS WITH ROPE

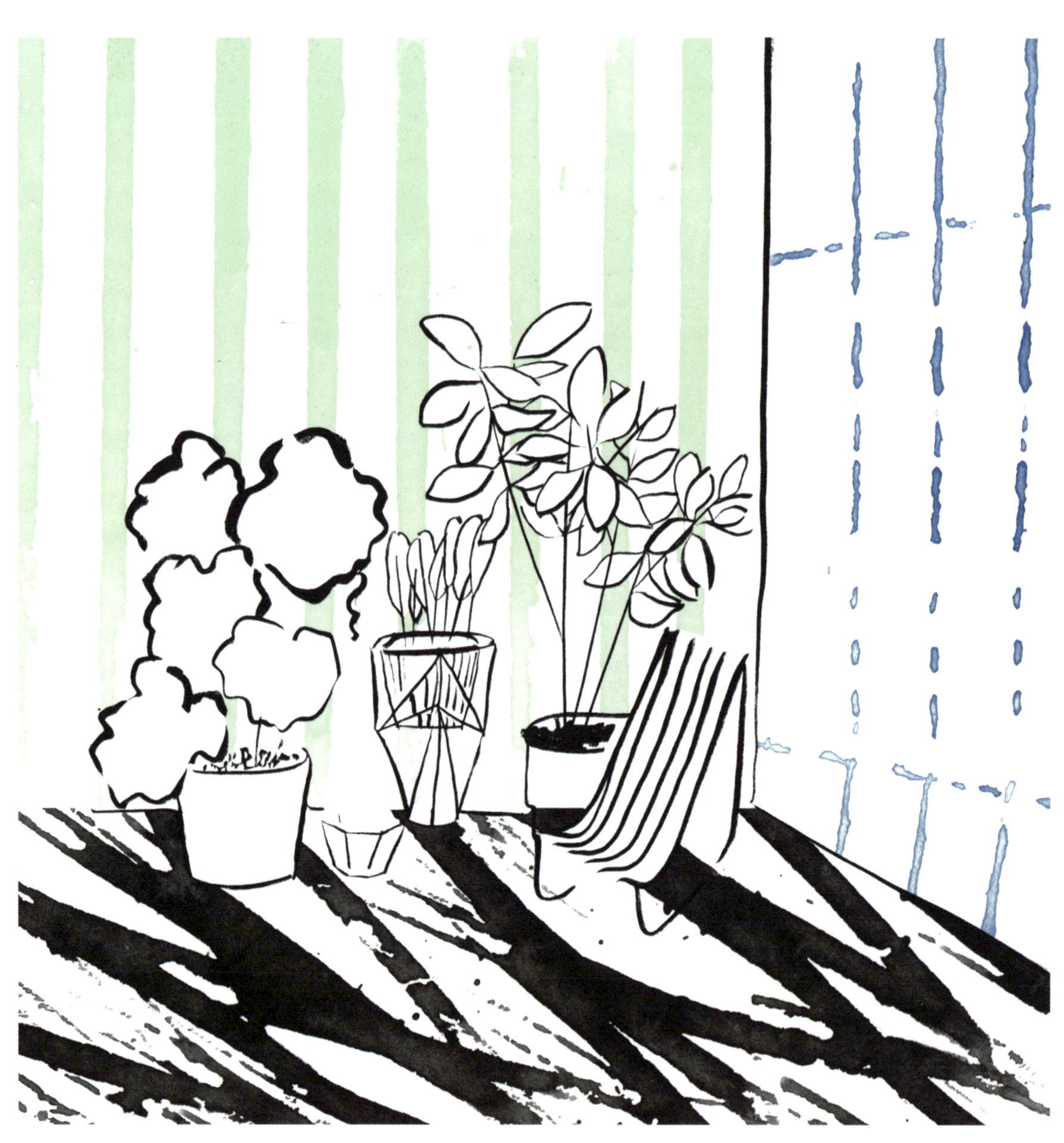

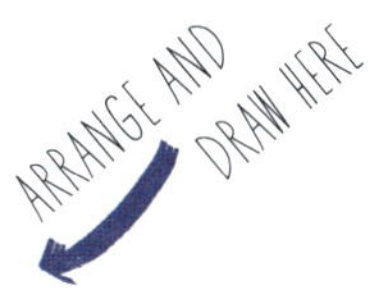

Take pieces of paper and different kinds of string. Now make a small puddle with ink and water in one of your mixing palettes or on a shallow plate. Hold a piece of string or ribbon by its ends, soak the center in the ink, and stretch the string onto the paper using it as if it were a stamp. Repeat the stamp process as much as you want to create line patterns and textures. Cut and arrange the printed pieces of paper above to create a composition and complete your artwork drawing on top of it with your pens.

TIP: COTTON ROPE OR STRING WILL SOAK BETTER THAN SYNTHETIC FIBERS IN THE INK. FEEL FREE TO ADD STRING TEXTURES TO A PAINTING INSTEAD OF MAKING A COLLAGE OUT OF SEVERAL SHEETS OF PAPER. FOLLOW YOUR INSPIRATION!

SHAVING FOAM MARBLING

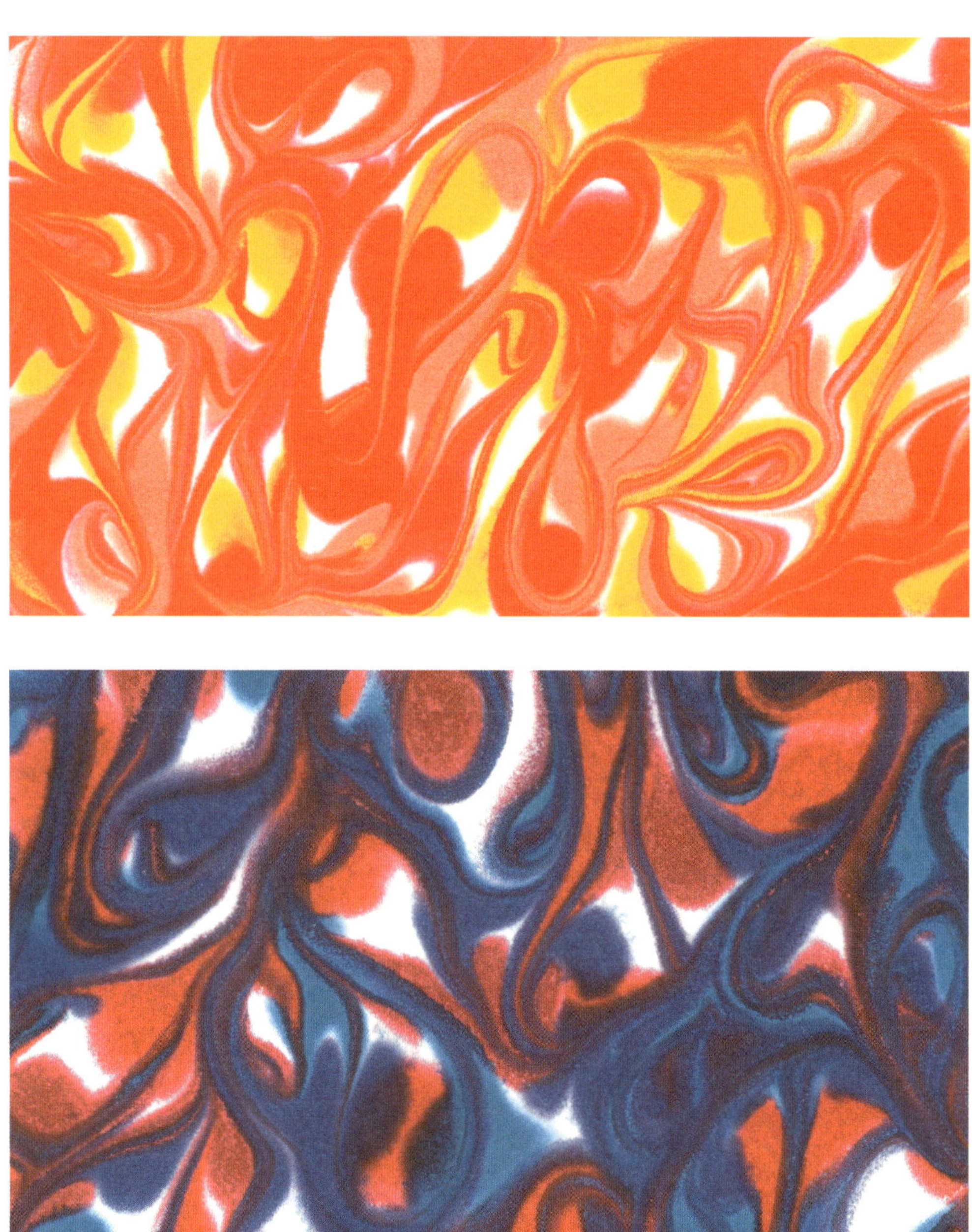

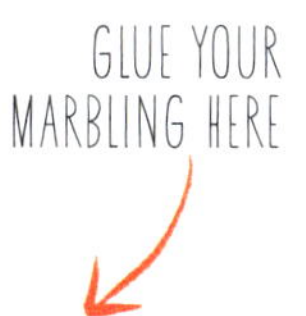

Shaving foam marbling is a faster and easier technique than the traditional one using carrageenan or methylcellulose. To experiment with it, spread an even layer of shaving foam in a flat container, add drops of ink on top of it, stir them around to create the marbled design, press a piece of paper on top to capture the color, remove the foam from the paper, clean it carefully with a squeegee, and let it dry. You can reuse the same foam a few times, removing the inked surface and smoothing it again.

TIP: PRESS THE PAPER ONTO THE INKED FOAM EVENLY FOR THE COLOR TO TRANSFER AS ACCURATELY AS POSSIBLE, AND BE GENTLE WHEN REMOVING THE COLORED FOAM FROM THE PAPER SO YOU DON'T DAMAGE THE DESIGN.

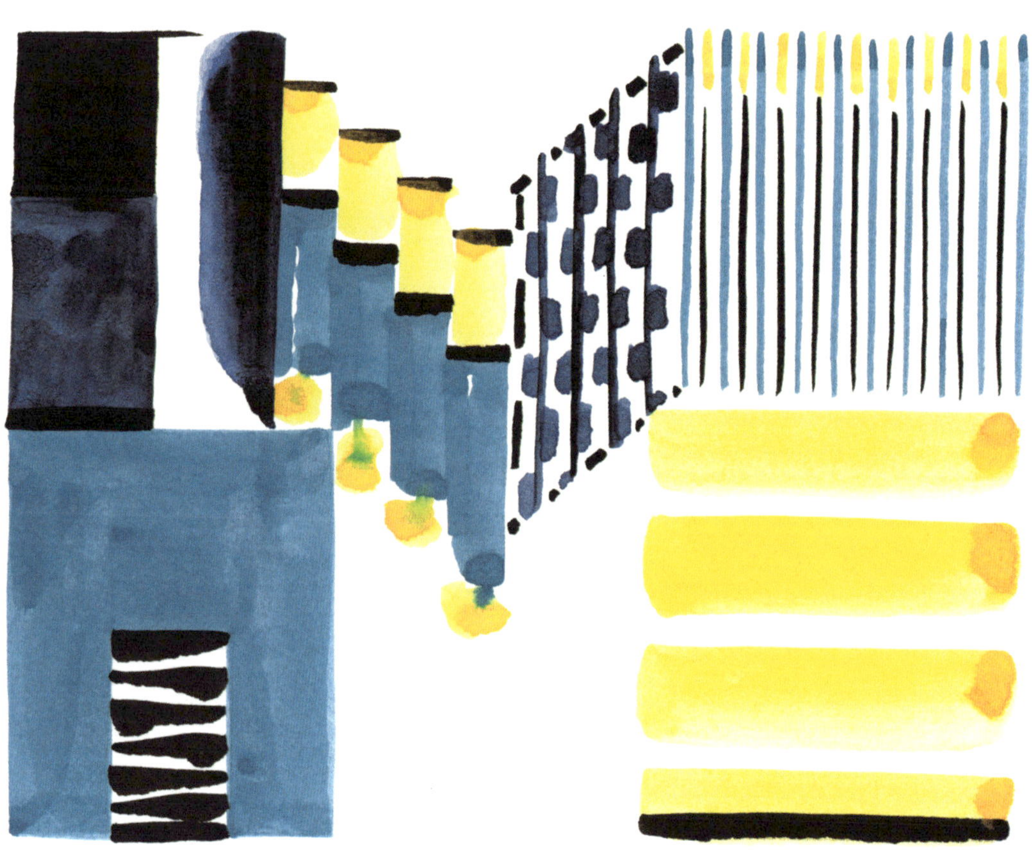

DRAW HERE

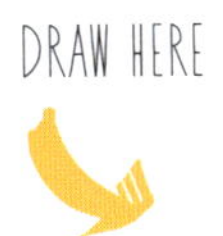

Choose a letter, such as your initial, one with a contour that you like, or anything else. Draw a frame for it with your pencil and ruler, if needed. Choose colors and start filling its shape with motifs and patterns that you like. They can be abstract, botanical, food-related—the possibilities are endless, so have fun!

TIP: ALTERNATIVELY, YOU CAN WORK ON A WORD THAT YOU LIKE AND CREATE UNIQUE LETTERING FOR THAT WORD. WHEN PAINTING IT, YOU CAN COMMUNICATE ITS MEANING OR JUST PLAY AROUND WITH COLORS AND SHAPES!

LANDSCAPE ABSTRACTION

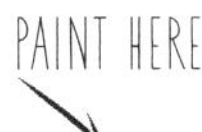

Paint a landscape as abstract as you can. It can be a city, forest, or any place you just made up. Don't be too concerned about being representational and keep in mind that just two areas of color can make an impressive landscape. Dive into Mark Rothko's colorscapes or check out Paul Klee's work for inspiration.

TIP: HORIZONTAL LINES ON THE BOTTOM OF YOUR COMPOSITION CAN GIVE THE ILLUSION OF WATER AND RECTANGULAR BLOCKS CAN COMMUNICATE BUILDINGS. TRY DIFFERENT BRUSHES AND PENS AND EXPERIMENT WITH THEIR SHAPES.

ALLOVER PATTERN

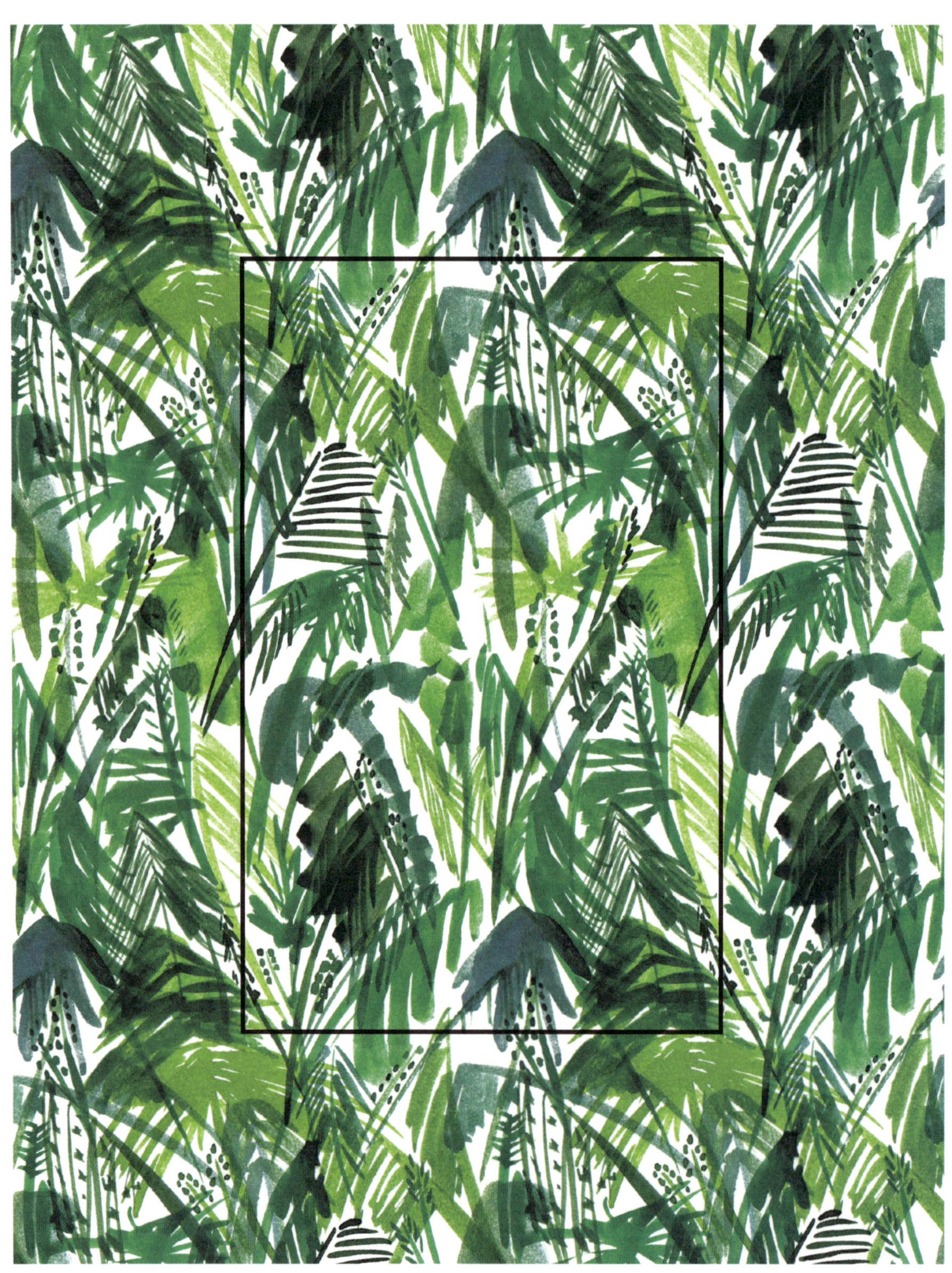

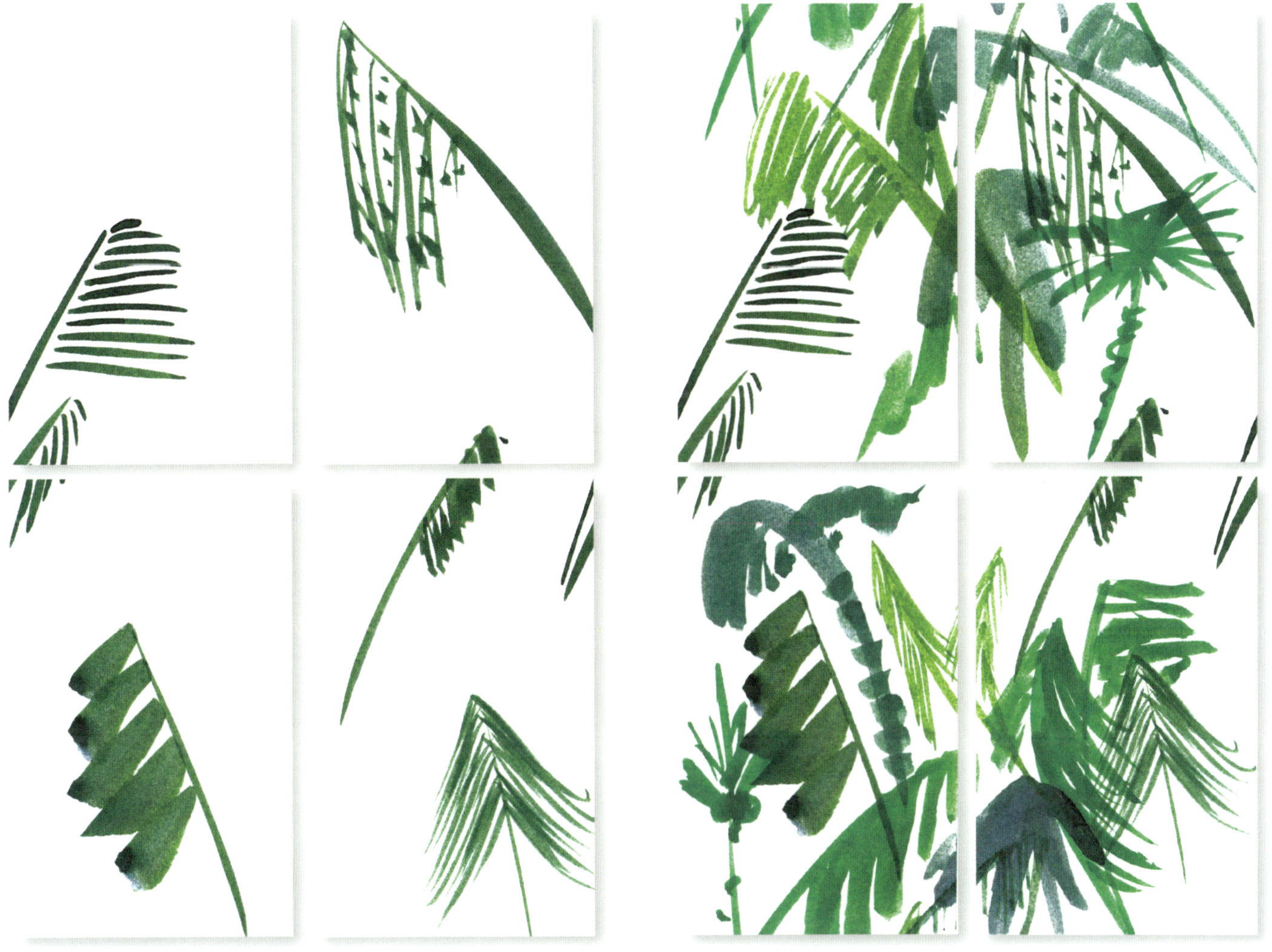

On a piece of paper, start painting and leave a wide margin of blank space around it. Using a ruler and craft knife, divide the paper into four equal parts. Cut out the four parts. Move the ones on the right to the left and the bottom pieces to the top. Join them by carefully applying tape to the reverse side of the paper. Complete your pattern by filling in the blank areas however you want.

TIP: FOR YOUR FIRST PATTERNS, YOU MAY WANT TO USE AN IMAGE EDITING SOFTWARE FOR THE REPEAT TO BE SEAMLESS. WITH PRACTICE, THE EDGES WILL LOOK MUCH CLEANER AND WON'T NEED RETOUCHING.

SELF-PORTRAIT

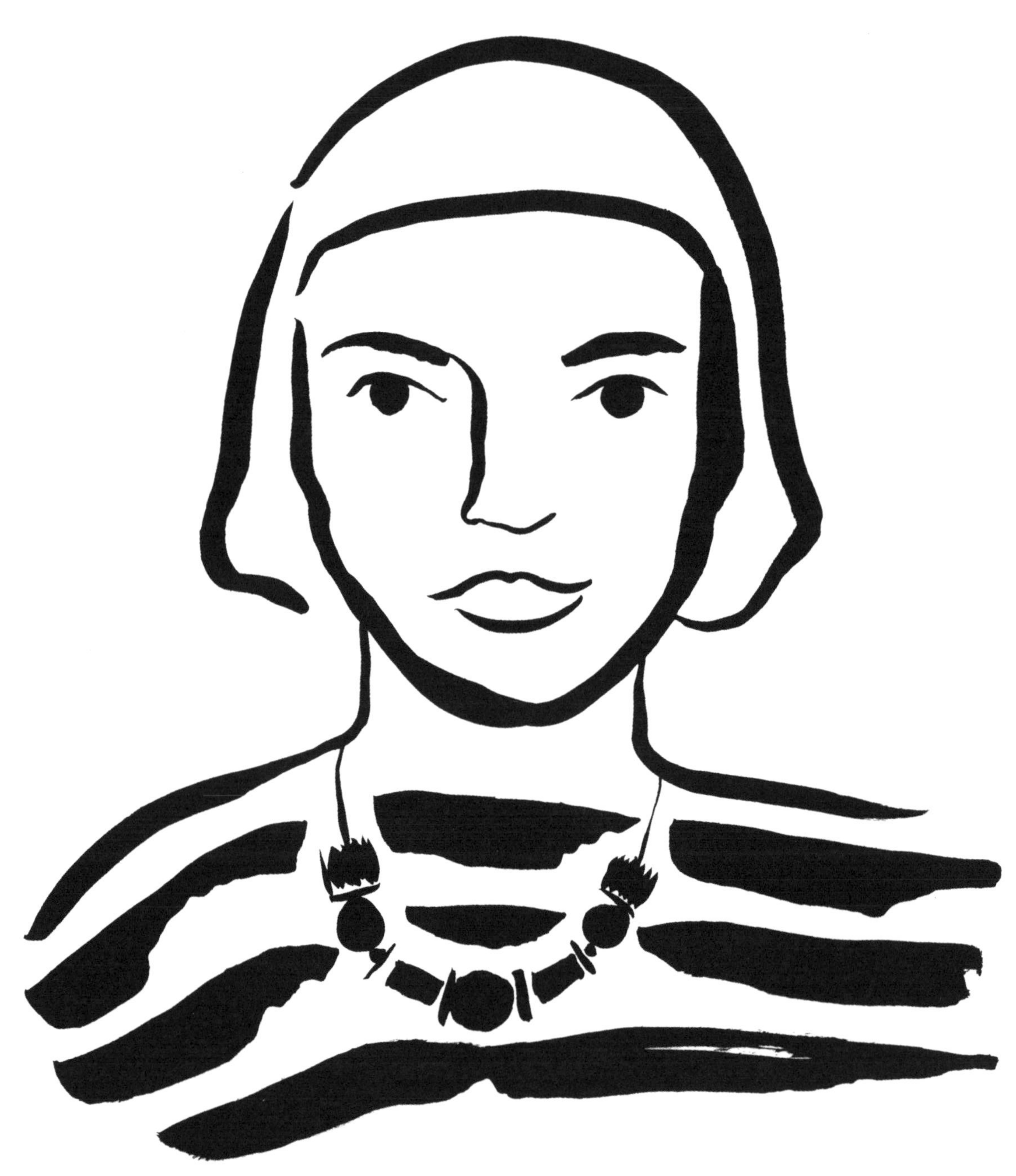

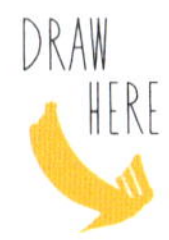

A self-portrait can be as free as you want. You can feel represented by a color, shape, collection of your favorite things, line drawing, and so on. It's a good exercise to make one from time to time to explore and capture your different phases and moods. To explore your features, get in front of a mirror and start sketching without being attached to the result. Use any of the techniques discussed previously and try to get to know yourself better with each painting. It's worth the effort!

TIP: IF YOUR IMAGE BRINGS UP SOME SELF-JUDGMENT, TRY MAKING YOUR PORTRAIT LOOKING AT A PHOTOGRAPH OF YOURSELF PLACED UPSIDE DOWN. THE FEATURES WILL BE MORE ABSTRACT AND YOU'LL BE ABLE TO FOCUS MORE EASILY.

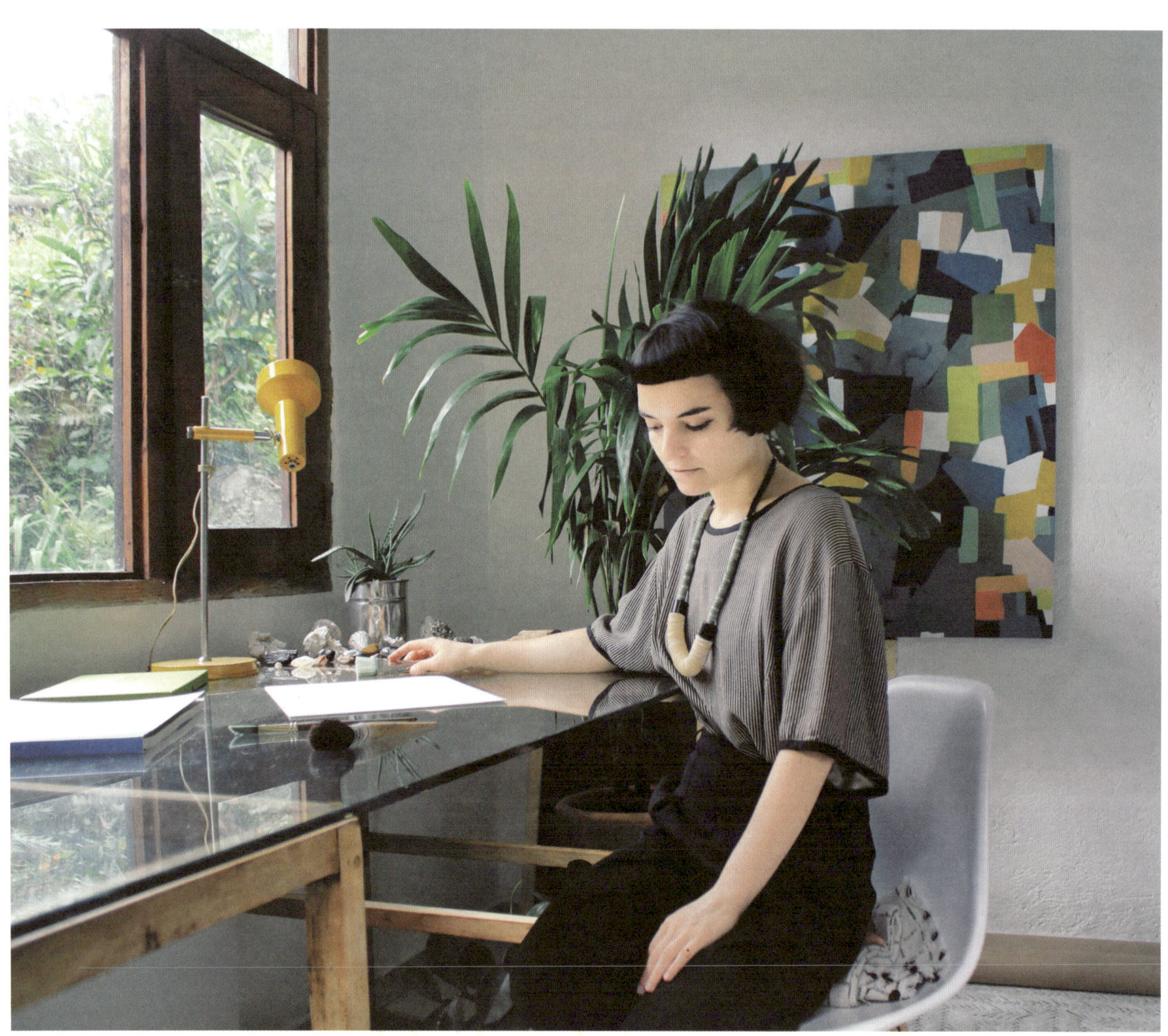

ABOUT THE ARTIST

Describing herself as a "professional enthusiast," Ana Montiel is quite a Renaissance woman. Her many passions and interests keep on piling up as years pass. Some of her influences are utopian architecture, eastern philosophy, antique botanical illustration, astronomy, quantum physics, the Bauhaus movement, and the Arts and Crafts movement.

With an education in fine arts, she kept on learning new skills, enough to set up a design studio in Barcelona; a wallpaper brand whose first product, "Topo Azul," was featured in the *New York Times*; a solid art direction and illustration career working on commissions for the likes of Anthropologie, Nina Ricci, and Clinique; exhibitions of her work in many countries; write two art guidebooks, *The Paintbrush Playbook* and *The Pencil Playbook*. Her daily life is full of experiments that often become more than that.

Ana spends her time painting, making pottery, cooking, designing all kinds of things, learning permaculture and ethnobotany, which she puts into practice in her own garden, and so on. "There's always something exciting to learn and try," she says.

Through Ana's latest ongoing art project, "Visual Mantras," she explores repetition as a meditation/trance and has developed a series of absorbing and richly colored geometries that bring up the cyclical rhythm of existence.

After spending most of her life in Europe, Ana decided to embark on a spiritual and artistic quest and moved to Mexico.

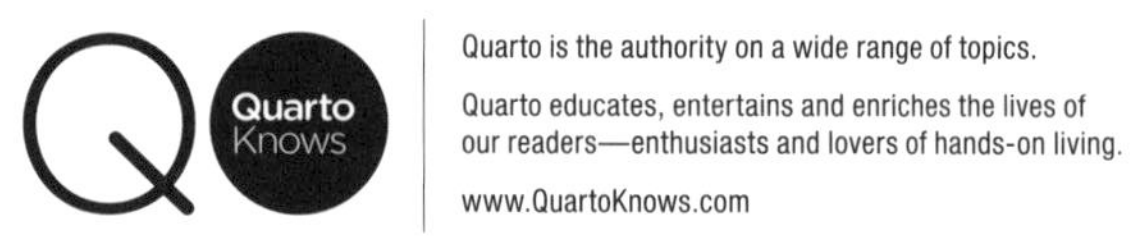

Quarto is the authority on a wide range of topics.

Quarto educates, entertains and enriches the lives of our readers—enthusiasts and lovers of hands-on living.

www.QuartoKnows.com

First published in the United States of America in 2016 by
Quarry Books, an imprint of
Quarto Publishing Group USA Inc.
100 Cummings Center
Suite 406-L
Beverly, Massachusetts 01915-6101
Telephone: (978) 282-9590
Fax: (978) 283-2742
QuartoKnows.com
Visit our blogs at QuartoKnows.com

10 9 8 7 6 5 4 3 2 1

ISBN: 978-1-63159-124-2
E-ISBN: 978-1-63159-189-1

Library of Congress Cataloging-in-Publication Data available.

Cover, design, and text: Ana Montiel and Tea Time Studio

Printed in China